SOUTHW
& ROCKY MOUN

VAIL 76

Denver 68

Aspen 80

Leadville 72

Dallas 100

Santa fe 90

AUSTIN
118

Houston 112

SAN ANTONIO
122

The New York Times

36

HOURS

EDITED BY BARBARA IRELAND

The New York Times

HOURS
USA & CANADA

SOUTHWEST
AND ROCKY MOUNTAINS

TASCHEN

Contents

Foreword

The stunning landscapes and wide-open spaces of the Southwestern United States and the Rocky Mountains deserve every bit of their worldwide fame. Out here, just about everything is on a grand scale, and that includes the jaw-dropping beauty. The peaks are extra high, the canyons extra deep, the sky the bluest blue. Strange is the topographical normal: mesas and buttes, salt lakes and salt flats, gigantic eroded rock arches. The cattle ranches cover thousands of acres, and the cactus can grow 60 feet high.

Hop around from city to city, and you'll find the experiences can be supersize, too, and accessible in just a weekend. No one does glitz better than Las Vegas or flaunts wealth with more panache than Dallas. Pack your Spandex and charge up your adrenaline for terrific outdoor sports: mountain biking, rafting, hiking, fly-fishing, and, of course, skiing and snowboarding. At the end of a long day on the trails or the slopes, work out the kinks at an opulent spa and satisfy your hunger with the help of a talented chef. If you're still not tired, hit a nightclub or drive out to where the city lights don't interfere with views of thousands and thousands of stars.

The independent spirit of the West thrives against the outsized landscape. Austin's indie music, Utah's Sundance Film Festival and imposing Mormon Tabernacle, Georgia O'Keeffe's visionary paintings, and Denver's nod to the unsinkable Molly Brown — all owe something to the limitless sense of possibility. So do the frankness and confidence of the friendly, fun-loving Westerners.

Native Americans, originators of pueblos and masters of adobe, are still leaving their mark. Latino influence is everywhere, in Mexican and Tex-Mex food, exuberant music, Spanish-speaking neighborhoods,

festivals, and textiles. Museums and galleries open up a fascinating past and display great art from the Old World and the New. Boutiques and galleries flourish in refurbished downtowns and gleaming new retail palaces. Cities flush with oil money have hired the world's most sought-after architects to embellish their skylines.

The 24 itineraries in this book lay out Friday-to-Sunday trips all over this fascinating territory. All are adapted — with updating, and often with new material specifically for the book — from the 36 Hours column in The New York Times, a travel feature that has been inspiring trips, wish lists, and clip-and-saves for a decade. Created as a guide to that staple of crammed 21st-century schedules, the weekend getaway, 36 Hours takes readers each week on a carefully researched, uniquely designed two-night excursion to an embraceable place. It guides travelers to an experience that both identifies the high points of the destination and teases out its particular character. From the beginning, 36 Hours has been a hit with readers.

In late 2011, The New York Times and TASCHEN published The New York Times 36 Hours: 150 Weekends in the U.S.A. & Canada, bringing 150 North American 36 Hours columns together in one volume. In 2012, the decision was made to offer this trove of travel guidance in another format: as five regional books, each easily portable and specifically focused, to meet the needs of a traveler who wants to concentrate on one area at a time. This book is one of the five; the others are devoted to the Northeast, the Southeast, the Midwest and Great Lakes, and the West Coast including Alaska and Hawaii.

The work of hundreds of writers, photographers, graphic artists, designers, and editors, combining their creativity over many years, has gone into 36 Hours and into this book. They are your guides on two dozen adventures in the American West — where to eat and shop, what to see and do, what not to miss — when you have just enough time for a weekend trip.

— BARBARA IRELAND, EDITOR

PAGE 2 Delicate Arch at sunset in Arches National Park outside Moab, Utah.

PAGE 4 The fantasyland skyline of Las Vegas, the uniquely American oasis of hope, abandon, and glittering.

OPPOSITE The Alamo, Texans' venerated symbol of their independent spirit.

Tips for Using This Book

Plotting the Course: Travelers don't make their way through a region or a country alphabetically, and this book doesn't proceed that way, either. It begins in a major city emblematic of the region and winds from place to place the way a touring adventurer on a car trip might. An alphabetical index appears at the end of the book.

On the Ground: Every *36 Hours* follows a workable numbered itinerary, which is both outlined in the text and shown with corresponding numbers on a detailed destination map. The itinerary is practical: it really is possible to get from one place to the next easily and in the allotted time, although of course many travelers will prefer to take things at their own pace and perhaps take some of their own detours. Astute readers will notice that the "36" in *36 Hours* is elastic, and the traveler's agenda probably will be, too.

The Not So Obvious: The itineraries do not all follow exactly the same pattern. A restaurant for Saturday breakfast may or may not be recommended; after-dinner night life may be included or may not. The destination dictates, and so, to some extent, does the personality of the author who researched and wrote the article. In large cities, where it is impossible to see everything in a weekend, the emphasis is on the less expected discovery over the big, highly promoted attraction that is already well known.

Seasons: The time of year to visit is left up to the traveler, but in general, the big cities are good anytime; towns where snow falls are usually best visited in warm months, unless they are ski destinations; and summer heat is more or less endurable depending on the traveler's own tolerance. The most tourist-oriented areas are often seasonal—some of the sites featured in vacation towns may be closed out of season.

Your Own Agenda: This book is not a conventional guidebook. A *36 Hours* is meant to give a well-informed inside view of each place it covers, a selective summary that lets the traveler get to the heart of things in minimal time. Travelers who have more days to spend may want to use a *36 Hours* as a kind of nugget, supplementing it with the more comprehensive information available on bookstore shelves or on the locally sponsored Internet sites where towns and regions offer exhaustive lists of their attractions. Or, two or three of these itineraries can easily be strung together to make up a longer trip.

Updates: While all the stories in this volume were updated and fact-checked for publication in fall 2011, it is inevitable that some of the featured businesses and destinations will change in time. If you spot any errors in your travels, please feel free to send corrections or updates via email to 36hoursamerica@taschen.com. Please include "36 Hours Correction" and the page number in the subject line of your email to assure that it gets to the right person for future updates.

OPPOSITE The Gold Hill Chutes in Telluride, Colorado.

THE BASICS

A brief informational box for the destination, called "The Basics," appears with each *36 Hours* article in this book. The box provides some orientation on transportation for that location, including whether a traveler arriving by plane should rent a car to follow the itinerary. "The Basics" also recommends three reliable hotels or other lodgings.

PRICES

Since hotel and restaurant prices change quickly, this book uses a system of symbols, based on 2011 United States dollars.

Hotel room, standard double:
Budget, under $100 per night: $
Moderate, $100 to $199: $$
Expensive, $200 to $299: $$$
Luxury, $300 and above: $$$$

Restaurants, dinner without wine:
Budget, under $15: $
Moderate, $16 to $24: $$
Expensive, $25 to $49: $$$
Very Expensive, $50 and up: $$$$

Restaurants, full breakfast, or lunch entree:
Budget, under $8: $
Moderate, $8 to $14: $$
Expensive, $15 to $24: $$$
Very Expensive, $25 and up: $$$$

Phoenix

With one of the fastest growth rates in the United States, Phoenix, Arizona, seemed to come out of nowhere to rank in the first years of the 21st century as the nation's fifth-largest city. Although the go-go trend came to a crashing halt when the housing bubble collapsed in 2008 and 2009, the city hasn't lost its appeal. The southern Arizona heat makes it an inferno in the summer, but the other nine months of the year are gorgeous and sunny. That means that three-fourths of the time, Phoenix, with its resorts, restaurants, contemporary shops, Southwest culture, and desert and mountain landscape, is perfect for exploring.
— BY RANDAL C. ARCHIBOLD AND AMY SILVERMAN

FRIDAY

1 *One Man's Castle* 3 p.m.

All sorts of people, some of them rich and famous, once flocked to Phoenix for health reasons, at least before smog became a big problem. But perhaps none was stranger than Boyce Luther Gulley, an architect from Seattle, who arrived in 1930 to recover from tuberculosis and, while he was at it, built a "castle" largely from found objects. The **Mystery Castle** (800 East Mineral Road; 602-268-1581), a trippy monument to Gulley's imagination, is adorned with all sorts of stuff, including tree branches for chairs, crooked windows, and Indian artifacts.

2 *Tacos and Mariachi* 6 p.m.

The border is just three hours away by car and more than a third of the city's residents are Latino, so Mexican food rules. Phoenicians argue over the best restaurants, but it is hard to top **Garcia's Las Avenidas** (2212 North 35th Avenue; 602-272-5584; garciasmexicanfood.com; $), a family-run restaurant known for its traditional menu and cavernous setting. A mariachi band often drifts from table to table, belting out ballads. No, the menu is not daring, but the plates come heaping with home-style favorites like tacos and enchiladas that won't damage the wallet. The juicy carnitas de puerco are worth a try.

OPPOSITE Saguaros at the Desert Botanical Garden.

RIGHT Phoenix sprawls out below a lookout point at South Mountain Park.

3 *Hollywood in Phoenix* 9 p.m.

The juggernaut of downtown construction in the frenetic days of the real estate boom—projects included a convention center expansion, a hotel, and condominiums—spared a few jewels, including the historic **Hotel San Carlos** (202 North Central Avenue; 602-253-4121; hotelsancarlos.com). Hollywood stars like Mae West and Marilyn Monroe stayed in this 1928 Italian Renaissance-style landmark, which still exudes an air of European refinement. Have a drink in the **Ghost Lounge**. The name is a reference to apparitions said to haunt the hotel, but it also feels right as homage to the bygone era that the place recalls.

SATURDAY

4 *Up Close at Camelback* 8 a.m.

Camelback Mountain sits in the middle of metropolitan Phoenix, and the Echo Canyon Trail in the **Echo Canyon Recreation Area** (phoenix.gov/recreation/rec/parks/preserves/index.html) is its most renowned hike. Locals call it the Scenic Stairmaster, and they'll warn you that this is no dawdle—the hike is 1.2 miles, and about 1,200 feet up, one way. On a clear day, you can see the Salt River Pima-Maricopa Indian Community to the east and Piestewa Peak (formerly known as Squaw Peak) to the west. You might also see cottontail rabbits, rattlesnakes, coyotes—and unfortunate hikers who didn't bring enough water (prepare yourself with a large bottle). For more child-friendly hiking, try some of the many miles of trails at **South Mountain Park** (phoenixasap.com/south-mountain-park.html), which

at 16,000 acres is sometimes called the world's largest municipal park.

5 *Hiker's Reward* 11 a.m.

Gaze up at the mountain you just conquered from a patio table at **La Grande Orange Grocery** (4410 North 40th Street; 602-840-7777; lagrandeorangegrocery.com; $). You'll fit in at this little fine-foods market and cafe whether you've showered post-hike or not. Look on the menu for the Jersey Girl Omelet made with pastrami

ABOVE Seclusion at the Royal Palms Resort.

BELOW Camelback Mountain rises up beyond the cactus at the Desert Botanical Garden.

and roasted potatoes. Or go vegetarian—there are plenty of good choices.

6 *Hiker's Rejuvenation* Noon

Step into the lobby of the **Arizona Biltmore Resort & Spa** (2400 East Missouri Avenue; 800-950-0086; arizonabiltmore.com) to appreciate the Frank Lloyd Wright-inspired architecture fully. Even on the hottest day, you'll instantly feel cooled by the structure of Biltmore Block, precast concrete blocks that make up the high-ceilinged main building. The Biltmore welcomes nonguests at its spa, so wrap yourself in a thick terry robe and head to a treatment room. (Reservations recommended.) Shopaholics may want to stick around afterward to seek out **Biltmore Fashion Park** (2502 East Camelback Road; 602-955-8400; shopbiltmore.com), a largely open-air mall stocked with high-end stores.

7 *Art Spaces* 2 p.m.

A cluster of galleries, boutiques, and restaurants in rehabilitated bungalows and old commercial buildings along once-forlorn Roosevelt Street have led to the area's christening as **CenPho**, the central Phoenix art district. Examine the local and regional contemporary art at **Modified Arts** (407 East Roosevelt Street; 602-462-5516; modifiedarts.org) and adventurous pieces at **eye lounge** (419 East Roosevelt Street; 602-430-1490; eyelounge.com).

Take a look at **monOrchid** (214 East Roosevelt Street; 602-253-0339; monorchid.com), which does double duty as an art space and a wedding venue. And walk around the corner to the front of **MADE Art Boutique** (922 North Fifth Street; 602-256-6233; madephx.com), which carries books, ceramics, craft items, and jewelry.

8 *The Original Residents* 3:30 p.m.

American Indian culture runs deep here, with several active tribes and reservations in the region. Just about all of them have contributed displays or materials to the **Heard Museum** (2301 North Central Avenue; 602-252-8848; heard.org), renowned for its collection of Native American art. The museum shop is also a great place to buy gifts.

9 *Eat the Unexpected* 7 p.m.

Phoenicians love a good meal as much as the next city slicker, and many flock to **Binkley's** (6920 East Cave Creek Road, Cave Creek; 480-437-1072;

binkleysrestaurant.com; $$$), where topflight contemporary American cuisine with a slight French influence can be enjoyed in golf shirt and shorts. Allow extra time to get there: it is 35 miles north of downtown Phoenix and traffic can be unforgiving. The mini-mall location may seem uninviting, but the chef, Kevin Binkley, is full of surprises. Examples: lobster bisque made with tangerines; black sea bream with daikon, pak choi, grapes, Fresno chile, and cilantro.

ABOVE The Mystery Castle, built by an eccentric architect using rocks, tree branches, and whatever was handy.

BELOW The pool at the Arizona Biltmore Resort.

and the servers wear "Alice eyes" makeup. Need we say more?

SUNDAY

10 *Remember Alice?* 10 p.m.

For a drink and a few helpings of eccentricity, drop in at **Alice Cooperstown** (101 East Jackson Street; 602-253-7337; alicecooperstown.com), named after the shock rocker and Phoenix resident Alice Cooper. You may find a live band or a boxing match,

ABOVE Alice Cooperstown, named for a favorite son.

OPPOSITE The Hotel San Carlos, built in 1928.

11 *Urban Desert* 10 a.m.

Driving through central Phoenix, you're more likely to see imported pine trees than saguaros, the giant native cactuses. The **Desert Botanical Garden** (1201 North Galvin Parkway; 480-941-1225; dbg.org) is the perfect place to get your dose of desert life without ever leaving a brick pathway. Spread across 50 acres in Papago Park, the garden is an oasis of towering cacti, aromatic flowers, and surprisingly verdant plants in the middle of the urban grid.

THE BASICS

Phoenix, 350 miles east of Los Angeles, is served by multiple airlines.

On the ground, a car is essential.

Royal Palms Resort
5200 East Camelback Road
602-840-3610
royalpalmshotel.com
$$$
Palms, gardens, and fountains help create a feeling of seclusion amid the Phoenix sprawl.

Arizona Biltmore Resort and Spa
2400 East Missouri Avenue
800-950-0086
arizonabiltmore.com
$$$$
Eight swimming pools, a golf course, and well-reviewed restaurants.

Sheraton Phoenix Downtown
340 North Third Street
602-262-2500
sheratonphoenixdowntown.com
$$$
A 31-story, 1,000-room tower that opened in 2008.

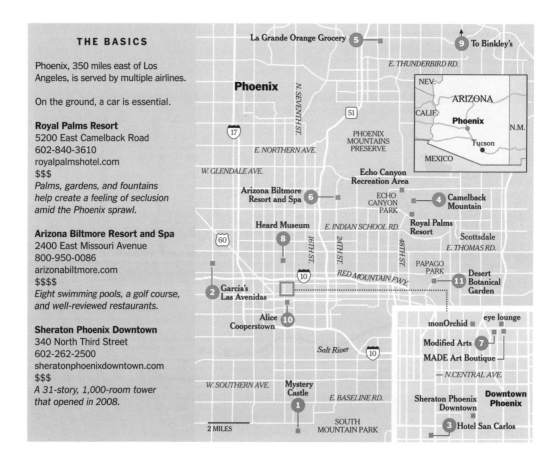

Scottsdale

It might be tempting a curse from the golf gods to enter the Scottsdale city limits without a set of clubs. But it's easy to spend a full weekend here far from the fairways. Just east of Phoenix, Scottsdale was once home to the Hohokam Indians; the town was founded in the 1880s by Winfield Scott, an Army chaplain who bought land to farm sweet potatoes. Today, Scottsdale is associated less with farming than with Frank Lloyd Wright, massage therapists, affluent second-home owners, and posh resorts. Wright's influence can be seen in much of the city's architecture as well as in his own Arizona headquarters, Taliesin West. Golf, if you wish. Or eat, explore, and then float in an infinity pool, contemplating your next cocktail.

— BY JENNIFER STEINHAUER

FRIDAY

1 *Enchilada Central* 7:30 p.m.

Much of Scottsdale may look as if it sprang up yesterday, but there are a few vestiges here and there of an earlier era. **Los Olivos** (7328 East Second Street; 480-946-2256; losolivosrestaurant.com; $), one of the oldest restaurants in the original area known now as Old Town, is still family run and has a personality all its own; the building itself looks like a piece of folk art, with a sculpture of a Mayan head rising from the roof. Inside, there's a lively central dining and bar area and a Blue Room that risks aquamarine overload. The food is solid Tex-Mex.

2 *Exotic Vintages* 10 p.m.

Kazimierz World Wine Bar (7137 East Stetson Drive; 480-946-3004; kazbar.net), known as the Kaz Bar, has all the trappings of hipness — no sign over the door (which is in the back), sofas, and a crowd of varying ages and sexual orientations. There are wines from dozens of nations available — yes, this is the place to find that elusive Thracian Valley merlot from Bulgaria. Expect live music or a D.J., too. Cavelike and dimly lit, Kaz Bar makes for good people watching.

OPPOSITE Spa splashing at the Fairmont Princess.

RIGHT The Old Town Farmers' Market, where local growers show off what a watered desert can provide.

SATURDAY

3 *A Plan over Pancakes* 9 a.m.

The coffee is strong and the banana buttermilk pancakes are yummy at **Cafe ZuZu** in the Hotel Valley Ho (6850 East Main Street; 480-248-2000; hotelvalleyho.com; $). Sit in the supermodern chairs or comfy booths and plot potential misadventures.

4 *Desert Produce* 10 a.m.

For a sense of how irrigation can make a desert bloom, mingle with the locals shopping at the **Old Town Farmers Market** (Brown Avenue and 1st Street; arizonafarmersmarkets.com). Along with the Arizona oranges and vegetables, expect a variety of other artisan and homemade products vying for your attention: apricot walnut bread, vegan desserts, barbecue sauce, bee pollen, cherry pepper relish, organic cider, tamales, hot doughnuts, and more.

5 *A Bit of the Old West* 11 a.m.

Stay in Old Town (roughly Second Street to Fourth Street, north to south; Scottsdale Road to Drinkwater Boulevard, west to east) for a stroll and a little browsing. There are scores of galleries displaying everything from works of the masters to American Indian jewelry to large contemporary paintings by local artists. You'll also find questionable Western-themed statuary, store names with puns (Coyo-T's), and the obligatory wind chimes and

dried chili peppers lilting and listing in the breeze. Check out **Mexican Imports** (3933 North Brown Avenue; 480-945-6476) for all the South of the Border kitsch you've always wanted. Of interest nearby is **Guidon Books** (7117 East Main Street; 480-945-8811; guidon.com), which specializes in out-of-print Western Americana and Civil War volumes.

6 *Then a Taste of the East* 1 p.m.

While you are in the neighborhood, do as the local residents do and hit **Malee's Thai Bistro** (7131 East Main Street; 480-947-6042; maleesthaibistro.com; $), a softly lighted room that muffles the sun-drenched action outside. The best bets are the tofu spinach pot stickers, Evil Jungle Princess (a pile of chicken doused in coconut cream with mushrooms and fresh mint), and the reliable pad Thai.

7 *There's Always the Rub* 3 p.m.

The ways to get pummeled, peeled, and rubbed in Scottsdale are endless, and there seems to be an almost Constitutional obligation to submit. From the shoulder rubs at the most commonplace hair salons to the aquatic watsu massage at the gorgeous **Sanctuary Camelback Mountain Resort & Spa** (5700 East McDonald Drive; 480-948-2100; sanctuaryoncamelback.com), there is something for every (reasonably generous) budget. Right in the middle is the **VH Spa for Vitality and Health** at the Hotel Valley Ho (hotelvalleyho.com), where the Back, Neck, Shoulders massage was heaven.

8 *Serenity, Inside and Out* 7 p.m.

Start dinner right at **Elements** (at the Sanctuary resort; elementsrestaurant.com; $$$) by angling for just the right seat on the patio at the Jade Bar, where you can watch the sunset while eavesdropping on first-daters as you munch on wasabi-covered peanuts. This moment is best paired with an Asian pear cucumber and ginger martini or a glass of sparkling rose. You will want to ask for a window booth inside the restaurant, where the chef cooks up seasonal fare as you take in Paradise Valley. The view is really the main course, but there have been some standout offerings on the changing menu, like grilled salmon, carrot and millet pot stickers, or a diabolical banana fluffernutter sundae. The Zen-like setting with stone and fireplaces is serene.

9 *Find the Party* 10 p.m.

Get a look at a Vegas-minded side of Scottsdale in one of the nightclubs near the W Scottsdale Hotel on East Camelback Road. **Axis-Radius** (7340 East

Indian Plaza; 480-970-1112; axis-radius.com) is a hot spot that draws young singles and aims to keep them dancing. The nearby **Pussycat Lounge** (4426 North Saddlebag Trail; 480-481-3100; pclaz.com), deals in density, packing partiers and their drinks into a small space. The **Suede Restaurant and Lounge** (7333 East Indian Plaza; 480-970-6969; suedeaz.com) seems to be aiming for a slightly more relaxing vibe.

SUNDAY

10 *The Architect's Place* 10:30 a.m.

Do not miss **Taliesin West**, the international headquarters for the Frank Lloyd Wright Foundation and the winter campus for the Frank Lloyd Wright

School of Architecture (12621 Frank Lloyd Wright Boulevard; 480-860-2700; franklloydwright.org). Troubled by poor health, Wright took up half-year residence in this 600-acre "camp" in 1937, and the complex was built by apprentices. Take the 90-minute tour, which takes you through the living quarters, working areas, and outdoor spaces that incorporate indigenous materials and organic forms. Then there's all that Asian art.

OPPOSITE ABOVE Taliesin West, built by Frank Lloyd Wright as a community of architects and apprentices.

OPPOSITE BELOW The rooftop pool at the Willow Stream Spa in the Fairmont Princess.

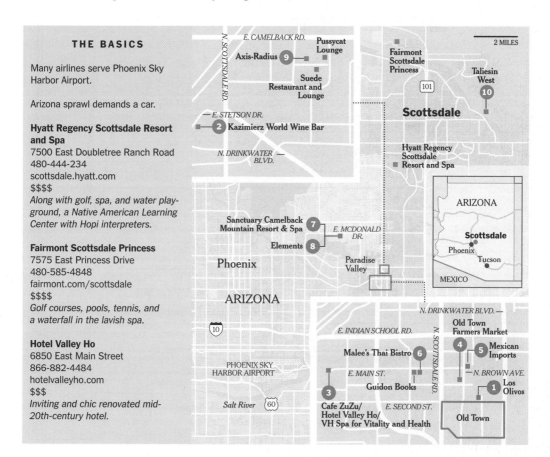

THE BASICS

Many airlines serve Phoenix Sky Harbor Airport.

Arizona sprawl demands a car.

Hyatt Regency Scottsdale Resort and Spa
7500 East Doubletree Ranch Road
480-444-234
scottsdale.hyatt.com
$$$$
Along with golf, spa, and water playground, a Native American Learning Center with Hopi interpreters.

Fairmont Scottsdale Princess
7575 East Princess Drive
480-585-4848
fairmont.com/scottsdale
$$$$
Golf courses, pools, tennis, and a waterfall in the lavish spa.

Hotel Valley Ho
6850 East Main Street
866-882-4484
hotelvalleyho.com
$$$
Inviting and chic renovated mid-20th-century hotel.

N. SCOTTSDALE RD.
E. CAMELBACK RD.
Pussycat Lounge
Axis-Radius **9**
Fairmont Scottsdale Princess
2 MILES
Taliesin West **10**
Suede Restaurant and Lounge
101
Scottsdale
E. STETSON DR.
2 Kazimierz World Wine Bar
N. DRINKWATER BLVD.
Hyatt Regency Scottsdale Resort and Spa
Sanctuary Camelback Mountain Resort & Spa **7**
E. MCDONALD DR.
Elements **8**
ARIZONA
Phoenix
Scottsdale
Paradise Valley
Phoenix
Tucson
ARIZONA
MEXICO
10
N. DRINKWATER BLVD.
Old Town Farmers Market **4** **5** Mexican Imports
PHOENIX SKY HARBOR AIRPORT
Malee's Thai Bistro **6**
E. INDIAN SCHOOL RD.
N. SCOTTSDALE RD.
E. MAIN ST.
N. BROWN AVE.
Guidon Books
1 Los Olivos
3
Salt River 60
Cafe ZuZu/ Hotel Valley Ho/ VH Spa for Vitality and Health
E. SECOND ST.
Old Town

Tucson

*Tucson, Arizona, has worked hard to shed its reputa-
tion as a tanning salon for retirees and snowbirds.
To complement its natural beauty — a national park
in its midst and mountains on four sides — the city
has poured hundreds of millions of dollars into its
downtown during the last decade. In lieu of adding
strip malls and high-rises, older buildings were saved
and retooled as movie houses and museums. And with
a deep-rooted Hispanic community, tides of Mexican
immigrants, and students from the University of
Arizona who never left after graduation, the city has
a youthful and multicultural glow.*
— RICHARD B. WOODWARD

FRIDAY

1 *Jet Age Graveyard* 4 p.m.

Tucson's bone-dry climate is easy on all kinds
of metal bodies. The city is a hunting ground for
used-car buyers as well as home to one of the world's
largest airplane graveyards. A sample of the 4,000
or so stranded military and civilian aircraft can be
viewed by driving along the fence on Kolb Road by
the Davis-Monthan Air Force Base. For a closer look,
the **Pima Air & Space Museum** (6000 East Valencia
Road; 520-574-0462; pimaair.org) offers tours with
frighteningly knowledgeable guides who can run down
all the specs on the SR-71 "Blackbird" spy plane.

2 *Hear That Whistle Blow* 6 p.m.

The Southern Pacific railroad reached Tucson
in 1880, and the moaning whistle of freight and
passenger trains can still be heard day and night.
For a front-row seat to the passing leviathans, head
Maynard's Market and Kitchen (400 North Toole
Avenue; 520-545-0577; maynardsmarkettucson.com;
$$). Less than 50 feet from the tracks, this dark and
handsome former depot attracts an upscale crowd
that comes for the extensive choice of wines (from
the store next door) and the reasonably priced menu.
Meat eaters enjoy the 14-ounce dry-aged New York

OPPOSITE Saguaro National Park, a favorite Tucson play-
ground when the summer sun isn't blazing.

RIGHT Terror remembered: a cold war artifact, the top of a
missile, at the Titan Missile Museum outside Tucson.

strip, and vegetarians the roast garlic and wild
mushroom stone-baked pizza. But just as inviting are
the sights and sounds of the rattling plates and glasses.

3 *Tucson Nights* 8 p.m.

Tucson has a jumping band scene on weekends,
a sleepier one the other five days. On warm nights,
the noise of music pumps through the open doors of
restaurants and bars along Congress Street. The center
of the action is often the historic **Rialto Theater** (318
East Congress Street; 520-740-1000; rialtotheatre.com).
A nonprofit showcase vital to downtown's renewal, it
books major acts but has no stylistic agenda.

SATURDAY

4 *Roadrunner* 9 a.m.

When the summer sun isn't blazing, Tucsonians
head outdoors. A prime destination is the **Saguaro
National Park** (3693 South Old Spanish Trail;
520-733-5153; nps.gov/sagu), which embraces the city
on two sides. To walk among fields of multi-armed
cactus giants, drive west about a half-hour along a
snaking road. Look for an unmarked parking lot a
few hundred feet beyond the Arizona-Sonora Desert
Museum. This is the start of the **King Canyon Trail**
(saguaronationalpark.com/favorite-trails.html),
put in by the Civilian Conservation Corps in the
1930s and the path for a refreshing morning hike. A
covered picnic area is at mile 0.9. Fitter types can
proceed 2.6 miles to Wasson Peak, highest point in
the Tucson Mountains.

5 *Modern Mexican* Noon

Tucson thinks highly of its Mexican restaurants, and one place that it can justly be proud of is **Cafe Poca Cosa** (110 East Pennington Street; 520-622-6400; cafepocacosatucson.com; $$$). Don't be put off by its location (in an ugly office building) or the décor (a vain attempt to import some glam L.A. style). The place has attracted national attention for a novel take on Mexican cuisine, which emphasizes fresh and regional. Try the daily sampler (El Plato Poca Cosa) of three dishes chosen by the chef. Expect an exotic mole and perhaps a zinger like a vegetarian tamale with pineapple salsa. Dinner reservations are essential for weekends.

6 *Picture This* 1:30 p.m.

One of the most impressive collections of 20th-century North American photographs can be found at the **Center for Creative Photography** (1030 North Olive Road; 520-621-7970; creativephotography.org), in a hard-to-find building on the University of Arizona campus. Containing the archives of Ansel Adams, Edward Weston, Garry Winogrand, W. Eugene Smith, and more than 40 other eminent photographers, it also runs a first-rate exhibition program.

7 *The Buy and Buy* 3:30 p.m.

Phoenix-style shopping has arrived at **La Encantada**, a mall in the foothills of the Santa Catalinas, with Tiffany and Louis Vuitton (2905 East Skyline Drive, at Campbell Avenue.; 520-615-2561; laencantadashoppingcenter.com). North of downtown at the **Plaza Palomino** (2970 North Swan Road), local merchants carry more idiosyncratic items like funky handmade jewelry and crafts.

8 *Eyes on the Desert Sky* 5 p.m.

The surrounding mountains are heavenly for star-gazing. The **Kitt Peak National Observatory** (Tohono O'odham Reservation; 520-318-8726; noao.edu), about 90 minutes southwest of the city and 6,900 feet above sea level, says it has more optical research telescopes than anywhere in the world. Aside from serving professional astronomers, it also has generous offerings for amateurs. One of these, the Nightly Observing Program, begins an hour before sunset and lasts four hours. An expert will show you how to use star charts and identify constellations and will give you a peek through one of the mammoth instruments. (Dinner is a deli sandwich; remember to wear warm clothing.) Reserving a month in advance is recommended, but you may get lucky and find an opening the same day.

9 *More Cosmos* 11 p.m.

For a nightcap, head to the boisterous **Club Congress** (311 East Congress Street; 520-622-8848; hotelcongress.com/club), on the ground floor of the Hotel Congress with five bar areas that offer steeply discounted drinks after 10 p.m. Live bands often have crowds of dancers spilling out into the lobby of the hotel. Finish the night at **Plush** (340 East 6th Street; 520-798-1298; plushtucson.com), where the acts are less polished but the drinks are almost as cheap and just as strong.

SUNDAY

10 *Early Bird* 9 a.m.

The **Epic Cafe** (745 North Fourth Avenue; 520-624-6844; epic-cafe.com; $) is a happening spot

ABOVE The control room at the Titan Missile Museum.

BELOW The Kitt Peak National Observatory. For nighttime stargazing, reserve well in advance.

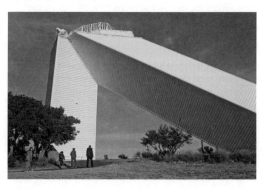

at almost any hour. This neighborhood hub on the corner of University Boulevard is open from 6 a.m. to midnight and serves an eclectic menu of sandwiches, sweets, and drinks to a clientele of laptop-toting would-be intellectuals and dog owners who jam the sidewalk tables. Grab a cup of the excellent coffee and a vegan seed cookie. If it tastes like delicious bird food, that's because it is.

11 *Missile America* 10 a.m.

For a terrifying yet educational reminder of the cold war, drive about 30 minutes south of downtown on Interstate 19 to the **Titan Missile Museum** (1580 West Duval Mine Road, Sahuarita; 520-625-7736; titanmissilemuseum.org). The nuclear silo housed a single intercontinental ballistic missile equipped with a warhead 700 times more powerful than the Hiroshima bomb. The museum tour lasts an hour. Much of it is underground, behind eight-foot-thick blast walls, and it ends with a peek at the 103-foot weapon, with its warhead removed.

ABOVE At Maynard's Market and Kitchen, in a former depot, glasses rattle as trains go by less than 50 feet away.

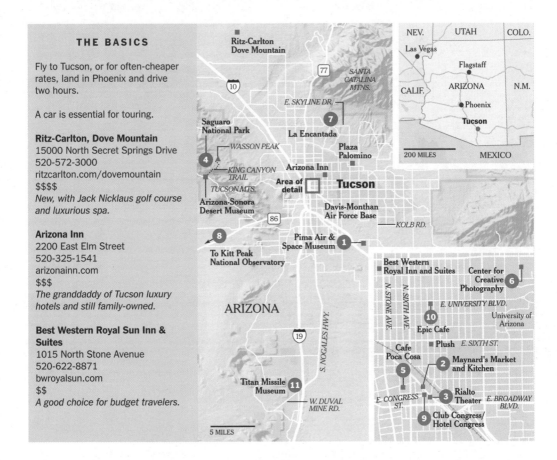

THE BASICS

Fly to Tucson, or for often-cheaper rates, land in Phoenix and drive two hours.

A car is essential for touring.

Ritz-Carlton, Dove Mountain
15000 North Secret Springs Drive
520-572-3000
ritzcarlton.com/dovemountain
$$$$
New, with Jack Nicklaus golf course and luxurious spa.

Arizona Inn
2200 East Elm Street
520-325-1541
arizonainn.com
$$$
The granddaddy of Tucson luxury hotels and still family-owned.

Best Western Royal Sun Inn & Suites
1015 North Stone Avenue
520-622-8871
bwroyalsun.com
$$
A good choice for budget travelers.

Sedona

Ask five people to sum up Sedona, Arizona, and you'll probably get five wildly different responses. Art lovers exclaim over the galleries specializing in Southwestern tableaus. Shopaholics rave about boutiques selling Western duds and American Indian jewelry. Pessimists rue the rash of T-shirt shops, while enlightenment-seekers wax spiritual about the "vortexes." And outdoor enthusiasts rhapsodize about hiking among red rock spires and ancient Indian ruins. All of this is great news for visitors, who can sample it all in a quirky city that some call the most beautiful place in the United States.
— BY KERIDWEN CORNELIUS

FRIDAY

1 *Red Rock Rover* 4 p.m.

Sedona's cinematic red rocks have been zipping across your windshield like scenes from a Hollywood western as you've driven toward town. Now it's your turn to ride off into the sunset. Turn up Airport Road to Airport Saddleback — you want the tiny parking lot on the left, not the chockablock Airport Vista farther up the road. Slip on hiking boots and hit the **Airport Loop Trail** for close encounters with the towering crimson sandstones: Bell Rock, Courthouse Butte, Coffee Pot Rock, and the Cockscombe. It's a 90-minute ramble, but if your energy flags, just turn back and scramble up Overlook Point, a good spot to watch paprika-red sunsets.

2 *Shopping for Dinner* 7 p.m.

It's hard to find authentic Southwestern food in Sedona, but there are good restaurants. One is **René at Tlaquepaque** (336 State Route 179; 928-282-9255; rene-sedona.com; $$$), where the dishes are main-stream — filet mignon, rack of lamb, duck with wild rice — but the quality is reliable. It's in the **Tlaquepaque Arts & Crafts Village** (tlaq.com), a Spanish-colonial-style shopping arcade with fountains and muscular sycamores. The shops and galleries are worth a look. Peek in the window of Kuivato Glass Gallery, which sells glass sculptures and jewelry.

3 *Wine by the Fire* 9:30 p.m.

Sedona isn't known for its night life. Most bars, in fact, shut down at 10 p.m. For a little art to go with your nightcap, swing by **Hundred Rox** inside the **Amara Resort and Spa** (310 North Highway 89A; 928-340-8900; amararesort.com). Sample a cocktail or a boutique shiraz from a 200-strong wine list as you examine a collection of paintings and sculptures culled from local galleries. The outdoor fire pit is just as picturesque.

SATURDAY

4 *Break an Egg* 9 a.m.

Kick-start your day in classic Sedona fashion with breakfast at the **Coffee Pot Restaurant** (2050 West Highway 89A; 928-282-6626; coffeepotsedona.com; $), which serves 101 "famous" omelets. Locals and tourists pack this kitschy joint, so you may have to browse the gift shop for jewelry and coffee mugs while waiting for a table. But once you're seated, the friendly waitresses are swift and might even leave the coffeepot on your table for convenient refills. Overwhelmed by the omelet choices? Try the hearty huevos rancheros, smothered in green chili. If you have kids, dare them to order the peanut butter, jelly, and banana omelet.

OPPOSITE The red sandstone rocks of Sedona.

BELOW The Chapel of the Holy Cross sits atop one of Sedona's famous vortexes, revered as sites of psychic energy.

5 *Sunsets, Pottery, and Frames* 10 a.m.
Galleries dot the city. The biggest of them is **Exposures International** (561 State Route 179; 928-282-1125; exposuresfineart.com), a sprawling space overflowing with paintings, sculpture, jewelry, and more. Check out Bill Worrell's prehistoric-art-inspired sculptures. Other interesting galleries can be found at **Hozho Center**, including **Lanning Gallery** (431 State Route 179; 928-282-6865; lanninggallery.com), which specializes in contemporary art. To learn more about the local art scene, visit the **Sedona Arts Center** (15 Art Barn Road; 928-282-3865; sedonaartscenter.com), a nonprofit gallery that holds exhibits and poetry readings.

ABOVE Rust-colored cliffs, shaded by oxidation of their iron-laced stone, tower above Enchantment Resort.

BELOW Earth Wisdom tours explore local history, geology, American Indian culture, and vortexes.

OPPOSITE Oak Creek, the gentle stream running through the valley that cradles Sedona.

6 *A Creek Runs Through It* 1 p.m.
Sedona is cradled in a fragrant riparian valley through which Oak Creek gently runs. Weather permitting, dine creekside at **L'Auberge de Sedona** (301 L'Auberge Lane; 928-282-1667; lauberge.com; $$$), a contemporary American restaurant with a stone patio perched at the water's edge. Indulge in grilled salmon or a tenderloin salad. Cottonwoods rustle, the creek burbles, and ducks waddle between the linen-draped tables.

7 *Spirited Away* 2:30 p.m.
You can't get far in Sedona without hearing about the vortexes, places where the earth supposedly radiates psychic energy. Believers claim that they induce everything from heightened energy to tear-inducing spiritual enlightenment. Whether you're a skeptic or believer, a guided tour of the vortexes by **Earth Wisdom Jeep Tours** (293 North Highway 89A; 928-282-4714; earthwisdomjeeptours.com) is definitely scenic. If vortexes aren't your thing, go

anyway. This tour also explores the area's history, geology, and American Indian culture, and there are other tours to choose from. You'll learn how the rocks became rust-colored: add a dash of iron, let it oxidize for several million years and voilà!

8 *Cactus on the Rocks* 6 p.m.

A prickly pear margarita — made from a local cactus — is the must-drink cocktail in Sedona, and one of the best spots to try it is the terrace at **Tii Gavo** at **Enchantment Resort** (525 Boynton Canyon Road; 928-282-2900; enchantmentresort.com). Tii Gavo means gathering place in the Havasupai Indian language, and in this restaurant well-heeled spa-lovers rub elbows with hikers fresh off the trail. Afterward, move inside to the **Yavapai Dining Room** (928-204-6000; $$$; reservations required for nonguests). The restaurant, with its American Indian pottery and views of Boynton Canyon, is no stranger to Sedona's celebrity visitors. The wine

list is extensive and far-ranging, but consider one of the local Echo Canyon reds.

9 *A Galaxy Far, Far Away* 9:30 p.m.

Thanks to strict ordinances on light pollution, the dark skies over Sedona are ideal for stargazing (or U.F.O. spotting). Take a cosmic journey with **Evening Sky Tours** (866-701-0398; eveningskytours.com). You'll be led by an astronomer who can point out those elusive constellations as well as an eyeful of spiral galaxies and the rings of Saturn.

SUNDAY

10 *Rock Your World* 6 a.m.

Soar over Sedona valley in a hot air balloon at sunrise for jaw-dropping views of rose-tinted buttes. **Northern Light Balloon Expeditions** (928-282-2274; northernlightballoon.com) offers three- to four-hour trips that include a Champagne breakfast picnic in a

remote spot (about $200). If you prefer to stay earth-bound, pack your own picnic and set out on the 3.6-mile **Broken Arrow Trail**. Buy a Red Rock Day Pass for $5; it allows entry to a number of natural areas and is available at most hotels and convenience stores. Hike along red rocks stained with desert varnish, weave through cypress forests, and climb up a doughlike outcropping for commanding views of Casner Canyon.

11 *Morning Spiritual* 10 a.m.

Peek inside the **Chapel of the Holy Cross** (780 Chapel Road; 928-282-4069; chapeloftheholycross.com),

a modernist icon that looks like a concrete space-ship jutting out of the craggy boulders. Designed in 1932 by Marguerite Brunswig Staude (but not built until 1956), the chapel is sandwiched between soaring concrete walls that bookend a gigantic glass window with a 90-foot-tall cross. Prayer services are held on Monday evenings, so don't worry about interrupting when you make your visit this morning. The chapel affords spectacular photo ops and another chance to have a psychic moment. The chapel sits on — you guessed it — a vortex.

ABOVE Inside Tlaquepaque Arts & Crafts Village, a Spanish-colonial style shopping arcade.

OPPOSITE Poolside relaxing at Mii Amo Spa is part of the outdoor desert ambience at the Enchantment Resort.

THE BASICS

Fly to Phoenix, rent a car, and drive two hours north.

Enchantment Resort
525 Boynton Canyon Road
928-282-2900
enchantmentresort.com
$$$
Adobe casitas, nature walks, a Native American culture program, and star gazing.

L'Auberge de Sedona
301 L'Auberge Lane
800-272-6777
lauberge.com
$$$$
Blends log cabin style with a touch of France.

Lantern Light Inn
3085 West State Route 89A
928-282-3419
lanternlightinn.com
$$
Attractive bed-and-breakfast with fireplaces, fountains, and patios.

1/2 MILE

ARIZONA

8 To Tii Gavo at Enchantment Resort/ Yavapai Dining Room

Sedona

Sedona Arts Center

Hundred Rox / Amara Resort & Spa 3

Earth Wisdom Jeep Tours 7

POSSE GROUNDS PARK

Coffee Pot Restaurant

L'Auberge de Sedona 6

Northern Light 10 Balloon Expeditions

— DRY CREEK RD.

4

89A

René at Tlaquepaque 2

Tlaquepaque Arts & Crafts Village

Lantern Light Inn

West Sedona

AIRPORT RD. —

9 To Evening Sky Tours

Lanning Gallery 5

1

Exposures International

SEDONA AIRPORT

Airport Loop Trail

Oak Cr.

179

Broken Arrow Trail

NEV.   UTAH   COLO.

Las Vegas

Flagstaff

Sedona

CALIF.   ARIZONA   N.M.

Phoenix

Tucson

CHAPEL RD.

Chapel of the Holy Cross 11

200 MILES   MEXICO

The Grand Canyon

More than a mile deep at its most majestic, the Grand Canyon can still drop the most jaded of jaws. The sun sparkling across the exposed rock, the delicate curl of the Colorado River, the birds chirping in the pinyon pines — and then a bus grinds past you on a hunt for the best postcards in the park. Yes, the Grand Canyon is big in every way, including the category of tourist trap. Over four million people visit this remote corner of Arizona each year, and the experience can be a bit death-by-gift-shop if you don't plan ahead — a necessity even if crowds and kitsch are your thing. During peak season, May through September, hotel rooms sell out months in advance, ditto for those mule rides, and certain rafting trips can be a year-long wait or more. Ah, wilderness!
— BY BROOKS BARNES

FRIDAY

1 *The Main Event* 5 p.m.

Save the best for last? Not on this trip. After driving the 81 miles from Flagstaff, Arizona, the destination where most air travelers land, head to **El Tovar Hotel** (Grand Canyon Village; 928-638-2631, extension 6380; grandcanyonlodges.com) The historic lodge, purposely built at such an angle that guests must leave their rooms to see more than a glimpse of the splendor, features one of the easiest access points to the canyon rim. Stretch your legs with a walk along the eastern portion of the 13-mile **Rim Trail**, which may leave you out of breath at 7,000 feet above sea level. Resist the temptation to go off the trail; park officials say about one person a year falls and dies and others are injured.

2 *Eat Hearty, Folks* 7:30 p.m.

El Tovar may look familiar — the exterior of the hotel had a cameo in *Vacation*, the 1983 road-trip movie. Clark Griswold, a k a, Chevy Chase, pulls up in his pea-green station wagon and robs the front desk. He should have at least eaten dinner first. The restaurant

OPPOSITE A lookout point along the Rim Trail at Grand Canyon National Park.

RIGHT The lobby at Bright Angel Lodge, one of the places to stay in the park.

at El Tovar (928-638-2631, extension 6432; $$$) is by far the best in the area. As twin fireplaces blaze, relax with an Arizona Sunrise (orange juice, tequila, and grenadine) and take in the wall-mounted Hopi and Navajo weavings. For dinner, start with a house salad with pinyon vinaigrette and then choose between the venison rib chops and beef tenderloin with wild shrimp for the main course.

3 *Star Struck* 10 p.m.

If dinner got a bit pricey, take comfort in a free show afterward. Because there is so little pollution here — the nearest cities, Phoenix and Las Vegas, are both 200 miles or more away — the night sky is crowded with stars. Pick up one of the free constellation-finder brochures in the lobby of El Tovar and gaze away. Bonus points for anybody who can spot the Lesser Watersnake.

SATURDAY

4 *Sunrise Sonata* 5 a.m.

The canyon's multiple layers of exposed rock are glorious in the morning light; download the soundtrack to *2001: A Space Odyssey* as a dawn complement — the combination heightens the experience even further. Take a morning run or walk along the Rim Trail heading west, and keep your

eyes peeled for woodpeckers making their morning rounds. Don't bother trying to make it to Hermit's Rest, a 1914 stone building named for a 19th-century French-Canadian prospector who had a roughly built homestead in the area. These days, it's — you guessed it — a gift shop and snack bar.

5 *Hop On* 10 a.m.

Those famous mules? Buy the postcard. The animals smell, walk narrow ledges carved into the canyon wall, and come with a daunting list of rules. (Reads one brochure: "Each rider must not weigh more than 200 pounds, fully dressed, and, yes, we do weigh everyone!") Join the modern age and tour the canyon aboard an Eco-Star helicopter, an energy-efficient model built with more viewing windows. There are several tour companies that offer flights, but **Maverick Helicopters** (Grand Canyon National Airport on Highway 64; 928-638-2622; maverickhelicopter.com/canyon.php) has a new fleet and friendly service. The tours are personal — seven passengers maximum — and are priced according to the length of the trip, with the longest being about 45 minutes at $235 per person. Ask the pilot to point out the Tower of Ra, a soaring butte named for the Egyptian sun god.

6 *Pack a Picnic* Noon

The nearest town and the location of the heliport, Tusayan, Arizona, is a disappointing collection of fast-food restaurants, motels, and souvenir shops. Get out of Dodge and pick up lunch at the deli counter tucked inside the general store at **Market Plaza** (located a mile or two inside the park gates; 928-638-2262). It's nothing fancy — pastrami sandwiches and the like — but it will at least save you from an order of junk food.

7 *Desert View* 1 p.m.

Hitting this tourist hotspot at midday will keep you clear of the throngs that assemble for sunrise and sunset. The view is still stupendous. From the historic **Desert View Watchtower** (26 miles past Market Plaza on Highway 64 East; scienceviews.com/parks/watchtower.html), constructed in 1932, you can see the Painted Desert, a broad area of badlands where wind and rain have exposed stratified layers of minerals, which glow in hues of violet, red, and gold. Park rangers give daily talks about the area's cultural history.

8 *Play Archaeologist* 3 p.m.

Outdoorsy types will want to do another hike — more power to them. For those who have had enough of the canyon for one day, another of this area's cultural treasures still waits to be explored. About 800 years ago, **Wupatki Pueblo** (about 34 miles north of Flagstaff on Highway 89; 928-679-2365; nps.gov/wupa) was a flourishing home base for the

Sinagua, Kayenta Anasazi, and Cohonina peoples. The remnants of 100 rooms remain, including a space that archaeologists identified as a ball court, similar to those found in pre-Columbian cultures.

9 *Who Screams?* 5:30 p.m.

If heights aren't your thing, relax: You've made it through the hard part of the Grand Canyon. Regroup after the drive back to civilization (or what passes for it here) with ice cream cones on the patio at **Bright Angel Lodge** (about two blocks west of El Tovar; 928-638-2631; grandcanyonlodges.com), which features an old-fashioned soda fountain. It no longer carries Grand Canyon Crunch—the coffee ice cream with caramel swirls and chocolate chip chunks was too expensive to manufacture in limited quantities —but try a strawberry shake. Inside the rustic motel is a newsstand, one of the few in the park.

10 *Dinner and a Dance* 7 p.m.

Apart from the dining room at El Tovar, Grand Canyon food can be alarmingly bad. But walk inside the Bright Angel Lodge and give the **Arizona Room** ($$) a whirl. The dishes are a mouthful in name — chili-crusted, pan-seared wild salmon with fresh melon salsa and pinyon black bean rice pilaf, for example — if not exactly in quality. After dinner, hang out around the stone fireplace in the lobby. With any luck, you will catch one of the randomly presented Hopi dancing demonstrations.

OPPOSITE The Wukoki Pueblo at the Wupatki National Monument near Flagstaff.

BELOW The Desert View Watchtower, built in 1932 and modeled after ancient towers of the Puebloan peoples.

SUNDAY

11 *Wild Side* 10 a.m.

Kaibab National Forest, 1.6 million acres of ponderosa pine that surrounds the Grand Canyon, is a destination on its own for nature lovers and camping enthusiasts. After saying goodbye to the world's most famous hole in the ground, stop on the way back to Flagstaff to explore the **Kendrick Park Watchable Wildlife Trail** (Highway 180, about 20 miles north of Flagstaff; wildlifeviewingareas.com). Elk, badgers, western bluebirds, and red-tailed hawks are relatively easy to see, along with short-horned lizards and a variety of other forest creatures. The Grand Canyon area is also home to scorpions, tarantulas, rattlesnakes, and Gila monsters — but those are (mostly) confined to the canyon itself.

ABOVE A Navajo hoop dancer performing in costume at the canyon's South Rim.

OPPOSITE Mule trains take tourists bumping down into the canyon along the Bright Angel Trail. Other sightseeing options include helicopter rides and rigorous hikes.

THE BASICS

Numerous airlines fly to Flagstaff, Arizona. Rent a car at the airport.

El Tovar Hotel
Off Village Loop in Grand Canyon Village
888-297-2757
grandcanyonlodges.com/
el-tovar-409.html
$$
By far the most upscale lodging in the area, centrally located and recently renovated.

Bright Angel Lodge & Cabins
Near El Tovar
888-297-2757
grandcanyonlodges.com/
bright-angel-lodge-408.html
$$
A cabin-style motel built in the 1930s that is bare bones but surprisingly comfortable.

Red Feather Lodge
106 North Highway 64
866-561-2425
redfeatherlodge.com
$$
As good a motel as any of the many in the Tusayan area.

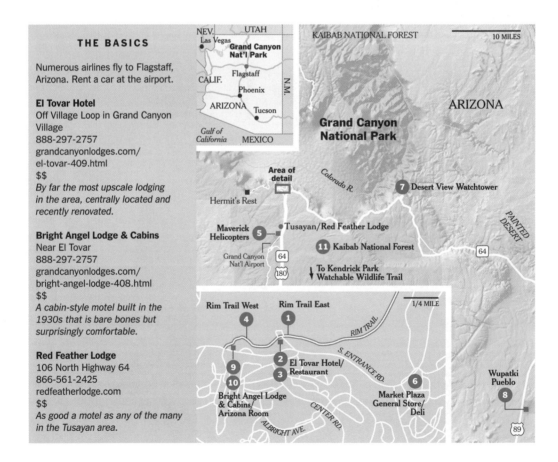

Las Vegas

The Las Vegas Strip grew fast in the first decade of the millennium, with new hotels, resorts, and entertainment palaces jockeying for attention. Even when hard times hit in the global recession, the building continued — two massive casino-hotel-retail projects, already on the way, opened their doors in 2010 although hotel rooms were empty all over town and the suburbs were hollowing out in the housing bust. The city was humbled, but that didn't stop its business people from hatching plans for new diversions, from a giant Ferris wheel to a gourmet vegan menu at the Wynn. Regardless of economic cycles, Las Vegas is never boring. And in the end, nothing beats a stroll along the Strip for a strong dose of America writ large and bright. — BY RANDAL C. ARCHIBOLD

FRIDAY

1 *Protein Palace* 7:30 p.m.

Start modestly. Guy Savoy at Caesars Palace and Alex at Wynn are among the higher-end restaurants in town, but look for a satisfying meal and a quick table without reservations at **Burger Bar in Mandalay Place** (3930 Las Vegas Boulevard; 702-632-9364; mandalaybay.com; $$-$$$$). It is a slightly upscale spot — you could pay $60 for a hamburger composed of ingredients like Kobe beef, sautéed foie gras, and Madeira sauce, among other delectable possibilities. But you don't have to. The restaurant lets you build your own burger using a cornucopia of ingredients, and most of them aren't so pricey. Then there's the Creamy Cheesecake Burger for dessert.

2 *Sgt. Pepper Does Vegas* 10:30 p.m.

Showtime. The pervasive **Cirque du Soleil** performances — half a dozen or more at different hotels — and the mammoth ads everywhere make Cirque something like the Starbucks of the entertainment circuit here. One of its extravaganzas, *Love*,

OPPOSITE The Las Vegas Strip, where ostentation can never be overdone.

RIGHT At the Mix Lounge in the THEhotel, part of the Mandalay Bay hotel and casino complex, the drinks may be expensive but the view takes in a lot of glitter.

a surrealistic, acrobatic take on the music of the Beatles (at the Mirage, 3400 Las Vegas Boulevard South), created a Vegas version of Beatlemania. It mixes snippets from original recordings and film clips with intriguing lights and shadows and, of course, a lot of oddly clad people floating and flipping around on wires, cords, and other devices. Somewhere in there lurks a story. Tickets for all of the Cirque shows are available at cirquedusoleil.com.

SATURDAY

3 *A Taste of Napa on the Strip* 9 a.m.

Try **Bouchon at the Venetian** (3355 Las Vegas Boulevard South; 702-414-6200; venetian.com; $$) for a French-themed breakfast in a Venice-themed hotel and resort. The restaurant is owned by the chef Thomas Keller, who made his name with the French Laundry in Napa Valley. A word to the wise: there are no reservations at breakfast, so if it looks like a long wait, ask for a seat at the bar. You get the full menu and often faster service. On one visit, custardy French toast arrived in a blink, as did a croque-madame with an eagle's nest of fries.

4 *Vegas at Tiffany's* 10 a.m.

If you've never experienced a shopping center designed by David Libeskind, here's your chance.

At **Crystals at CityCenter** (3720 South Las Vegas Boulevard; crystalsatcitycenter.com), retailers purvey their wares inside what looks like — yes — a cluster of gigantic crystals. Here you can find Tiffany's, Prada, Cartier, Fendi, Versace, and others of their kind, along with a Wolfgang Puck pizzeria, together in one eye-popping setting. It's one element of the huge new CityCenter development, a set of gleaming towers you won't be able to overlook. A smaller, somewhat less pricey collection of new shops is in the Strip's other giant new development, the Cosmopolitan. You don't have to buy to appreciate the spectacle.

5 *The Demi-Eiffel* 1 p.m.

To drink in views of the Strip, many people head to the **Stratosphere Tower**, a 1,149-foot spire (2000 Las Vegas Boulevard South; 702-380-7711; stratospherehotel.com) that has a fine restaurant near the top. But the center of the strip offers an appealing alternative, the **Eiffel Tower** of the **Paris Las Vegas** hotel (3655 Las Vegas Boulevard South; 702-946-7000; parislasvegas.com). It's as close to the real thing as, well, the New York-New York hotel and casino is to that little burg on the Hudson. But at 460 feet, less than half as tall as the original, you see the

Strip and surrounding mountains plus a bonus bird's-eye view of the periodic ultrafountain show outside the Bellagio. It is even more entrancing at night.

6 *Tea and Crustaceans* 2:30 p.m.

A lot of hotel restaurants these days offer afternoon tea. The **Petrossian Bar** at the Bellagio (3600 Las Vegas Boulevard South; 702-693-7111; bellagio.com; $$$) is typical, and it's a lot more than finger sandwiches and crumpets. Expect Maine lobster, pico de gallo, and caviar served open-faced on a brioche. Get a seat outside the main room to watch the parade of people stream through the lobby.

7 *Luck Be a Lady* 4 p.m.

Oh, yeah. Gambling. The new casinos beckon, but consider the slightly older **Wynn Las Vegas** (3131 Las Vegas Boulevard South; 702-770-7000; wynnlasvegas.com), particularly the elbow-to-elbow poker room. Riding the burst of intense interest in the game, several hotel casinos have made more room for pokerphiles. Even if you don't play, just watching the action and checking out the Runyonesque characters who come and go is entertainment enough. And just a few steps away, right in the hotel, is a luxury car dealership, Penske-Wynn Ferrari/Maserati (penskewynn.com). There's a fee just to walk inside, but that shouldn't even make you blink, what with all your poker winnings.

ABOVE The Crystals at CityCenter, a retail complex with Tiffany's, Prada, and a Wolfgang Puck pizzeria.

8 *That Old-Time Linguine* 7 p.m.

Get some distance from the Strip's hurly-burly. The **Bootlegger Bistro** (7700 Las Vegas Boulevard South; 702-736-4939; bootleggerlasvegas.com; $$-$$$), an old-fashioned Italian restaurant, dates to 1949, making it practically prehistoric in Las Vegas years. It sits beyond the southern glut of Strip hotels, but it's worth the trip. Its dimly lighted interior of cherry red and dark wood, along with all the celebrity photographs on the walls, evokes the ancient, loungy Vegas. Most nights include live music, sometimes with big-name musicians taking a break from their gigs in the arenas farther north. The house special is seafood del diavolo.

9 *Luck on the Lanes* 9 p.m.

You can catch some live jazz in the **Rocks Lounge** of the new-not-so-long-ago **Red Rock Casino, Resort & Spa** (11011 West Charleston Boulevard; 702-797-7777; redrocklasvegas.com), but when you tire of the shows, there's another option here: go bowling at **Red Rock Lanes** (redrocklanes.com). A luxury bowling center (that's its own description), it has 72 lanes, LCD scoring monitors, lounge service, and Saturday-night cosmic bowling, featuring light-show effects, fog machines, glow-in-the-dark alleys and balls, and pounding music to enjoy it all by.

ABOVE A performance of Cirque du Soleil's Beatles-based show at the Mirage.

BELOW Blackjack tables at the Cosmopolitan. Gambling is still at the heart of it all.

SUNDAY

10 *Desert Respite* 11 a.m.

A one-hour drive from Las Vegas, at the northern end of Lake Mead, is **Valley of Fire State Park** (Interstate 15, Exit 75, Overton; 702-397-2088; parks.nv.gov/vf.htm). Its name comes from the red sandstone formations, but if you travel there in summer you might think otherwise. The rest of the year, it makes for a pleasant trip, with plenty of trails and majestic desert scenery. The open expanses of desert, pocked with otherworldly, towering rock formations, recall Martian landscapes as photographed by NASA. Arch Rock and Poodle Rock are particularly captivating and are accessible from main roads or trails. Beware, or join, the Trekkies: Silica Dome off Fire Creek Road was the setting for the planet where James T. Kirk fell to his death in *Star Trek: Generations.* Mourners still beam themselves there.

ABOVE Valley of Fire State Park, near Lake Mead.

OPPOSITE A downsized Eiffel Tower and Arc de Triomphe at the Paris Las Vegas hotel.

THE BASICS

Las Vegas is a four-hour drive from Los Angeles. Its airport is served by the major airlines. At the Strip, walk or use taxis, buses, and the monorail. Elsewhere, drive a car.

The Cosmopolitan
3708 Las Vegas Boulevard South
702-215-5500
cosmopolitanlasvegas.com
$$$
In a new multibillion-dollar development, with hotel interiors designed by David Rockwell.

Aria Resort and Casino
3730 Las Vegas Boulevard South, in CityCenter
702-590-7111
arialasvegas.com
$$$
In CityCenter, new in 2009, with 4,000 rooms and every amenity (some with extra fees).

Luxor
3900 Las Vegas Boulevard South
702-262-4444
luxor.com
$$
Bargain-hunters could do worse.

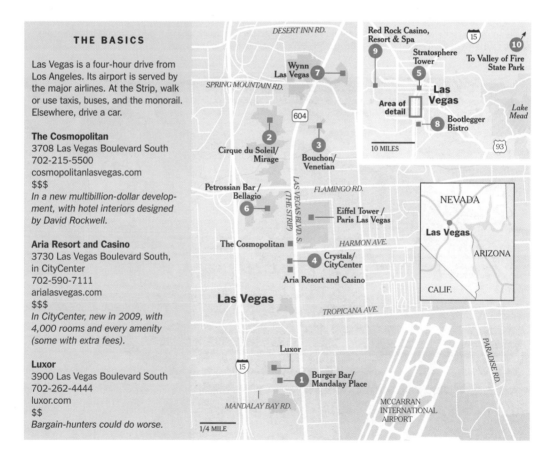

Moab

It's hard not to become a dime-store philosopher in Moab, Utah. With its dipping green valleys and great red rocks piercing the wide blue sky, this tiny Utah town can be a heady study in perspective. One minute you're sipping coffee on Main Street, tucked safely between the wild, barren Canyonlands National Park and the magnificent stony surrealism of Arches National Park. A short drive later, you're thousands of dizzying feet above civilization, the wind whipping you senseless. The startling beauty of this terrain is enough to leave even the most seasoned traveler frozen in the sand, blinking in disbelief.

— BY CINDY PRICE

FRIDAY

1 *A Delicate Balance* 3 p.m.

You can look at a million photos of the **Delicate Arch** (and you will), but nothing prepares you for the real deal. At **Arches National Park** (Highway 191; 435-719-2299; nps.gov/arch), take the mile-and-a-half hike up steep, uneven slick rock to hit the landmark just before sunset (bring a flashlight and plenty of water). The arch doesn't come into view until the last second, and when it does, it's unforgettable. Perched on the brink of an enormous sandstone bowl, you can edge your way around and stand beneath the massive arch for a picture, but be forewarned — though the ground there is wider than a big-city sidewalk, the combination of steep dropoff, gusty wind, and gleaming sun makes for a dizzying few seconds.

2 *The Barroom Floor* 8 p.m.

It's no Las Vegas, but Moab can kick it. Swing by **La Hacienda** (574 North Main Street; 435-259-6319; $), a townie favorite, for tasty fried fish tacos. Then hit **World Famous Woody's Tavern** (221 South Main Street; myspace.com/worldfamouswoodystavern), where everyone from local hipsters to vacationing Dutch couples pull on cold drafts. Some say the floor is painted red to cover up bloodstains from brawls,

OPPOSITE The Delicate Arch, perched on the brink of an enormous sandstone bowl at Arches National Park.

RIGHT After a uranium mining bust in the 1980s, Moab reinvented itself as an outdoor recreation spot.

but don't be put off — aside from foosball, Woody's is fairly docile these days.

SATURDAY

3 *Rough Riders* 8:30 a.m.

There are gentler ways to take in the lay of the land, but some scenic tours are just too tame. At the **Moab Adventure Center** (225 South Main Street; 435-259-7019; moabadventurecenter.com), you can book a Hummer Safari — a guide does the driving — that will take you in and out of rock canyons and up rough and steep sandstone hills (don't think about what it's going to be like coming down). Moab is also popular with mountain bikers — if that's your thing, check out **Moab Cyclery** (391 Main Street; 435-259-7423; moabcyclery.com) or another local bike outfitter for rentals and day trips.

4 *Old School* 12:30 p.m.

In a town where scenery looms large, it's easy to drive past the unassuming **Milt's Stop & Eat** (356 South 400 East; 435-259-7424; miltsstopandeat.com; $). But this little diner, which has been doling out fresh chili and shakes since 1954, comes through where it counts. Pull up to the counter and order a mouthwatering double bacon cheeseburger. It's a greasy-spoon chef-d'oeuvre, with aged-beef patties and thick slices of smoked bacon. A creamy chocolate malt will have you cursing the advent of frozen yogurt.

5 *Hole Sweet Hole* 1:30 p.m.

In 1945, Albert Christensen built his wife, Gladys, the home of their dreams — in the middle of a rock. Part kitsch memorial, part love story, **Hole N" the Rock** (11037 South Highway 191; 435-686-2250; theholeintherock.com) is surely a tourist trap, but a heartwarming one. Even the steady drone of the

ABOVE Main Street and its rugged backdrop.

BELOW Heading for a cold draft at Woody's Tavern.

OPPOSITE ABOVE A heartwarming tourist trap.

OPPOSITE BELOW A sunset over Moab.

gum-smacking guide on your tour can't dispel the sheer marvel of this 5,000-square-foot testament to one man's obsession. It took Albert 12 years to hand-drill the place, and Gladys another eight to give it a woman's touch. Each room is lovingly preserved with knick-knacks or Albert's taxidermy. Outside, wander over to the inexplicable but equally delightful petting zoo filled with llamas, emus, and wallabies.

6 *Main Street* 3:30 p.m.

Like most small towns with attitude, Moab has a main street that's pretty darn cute. Start your walk with an iced coffee and a fresh slice of quiche at **EklectiCafé** (352 North Main Street; 435-259-6896; $). For a quick lesson on local topography, check out the area relief map at the **Museum of Moab** (118 East Center Street; 435-259-7985; moabmuseum.org). The artifacts on display include dinosaur bones and tracks, ancient pottery, mining tools, and a proud pioneer's piano — all part of the Moab story.

7 *World's Biggest Stage Set* 6 p.m.

Head out of town, hang a right at Scenic Byway 128, drive 18 miles, and take a right on La Sal Mountain Road toward Castle Valley. The pretty, winding route leads to **Castle Rock**—a dead ringer for Disney's Big Thunder Mountain Railroad and the star of old Chevrolet commercials. Turn around at Castleton Tower and drop into **Red Cliffs Lodge** (Mile Post 14, Highway 128; 435-259-2002; redcliffslodge.com) for a free wine tasting at the **Castle Creek Winery**. Afterward, check out the **Movie Museum** in the basement—a small homage to the many films shot in Moab, including *Rio Grande* and *Indiana Jones and the Last Crusade*.

8 *Local Brew* 8 p.m.

You've tasted the wine. Now sample the ale. The **Moab Brewery** (686 South Main Street; 435-259-6333; themoabbrewery.com; $) has a variety of hearty brews, plus its own homemade root beer. The dinner menu has plenty of beef and chicken, including barbecue, balanced by a cheese-heavy "Very Veggie" section and a promise that the frying is done in zero-trans-fat oil.

SUNDAY

9 *Dawn on the Cliffs* 7 a.m.

There are few reasons to endorse waking up at 7 on a Sunday, but a sunrise at Dead Horse Point passes the test. Hit the **Wicked Brew Drive Thru** (132 North Main Street; 435-259-0021; wickedbrewmoab.com) for an espresso-laced eye opener, and then take the winding drive up Route 313 to the 2,000-foot vantage point at **Dead Horse Point State Park** (435-259-2614;

utah.com/stateparks/dead_horse.htm). Watch the sun break over the vast, beautiful Canyonlands. To the west, look for Shafer Trail, the dusty road where Thelma and Louise sealed their fate in the 1991 Ridley Scott film.

10 *Rapid Observations* 10:30 a.m.

In the '70s, before Moab became known as the mountain-biking capital of the world, whitewater rafting was the big buzz. **Red River Adventures** (1140 South Main Street; 435-259-4046; redriveradventures.com)

offers trips that take it easy through Class II and III rapids, and others that go for Class IV. If you'd rather try a different form of sightseeing, the company also offers rock climbing and horseback trips.

ABOVE Scenery looms large for Moab, tucked between Canyonlands and Arches National Parks.

OPPOSITE Cycling along Scenic Byway 128 outside of town. The local terrain is legendary among mountain bikers, and outfitters in Moab will provide bicycles and gear.

THE BASICS

Fly to Salt Lake City, rent a car, and drive 235 scenic miles southeast to Moab.

Sunflower Hill Inn
185 North 300 East
435-259-2974
sunflowerhill.com
$$
Lovely restored inn with 12 rooms.

Gonzo Inn
100 West 200 South
435-259-2515
gonzoinn.com
$$
Colorful retro-style hotel.

Red Cliffs Lodge
Mile Post 14, Highway 128
435-259-2002
redcliffslodge.com
$$-$$$
Overlooking the Colorado River 20 minutes out of town.

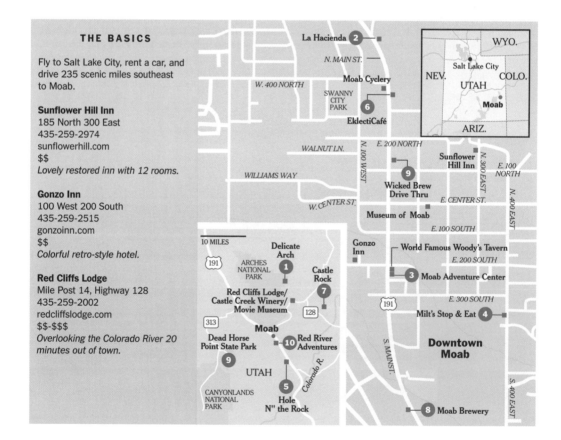

Salt Lake City

Sprawling and rapidly growing, Salt Lake City, Utah, is more complicated and cosmopolitan than most outsiders know. It's also more beautiful. Situated directly below the towering Wasatch Front, the city has a spectacular natural backdrop, beautiful 1900s neighborhoods, and one of the nation's most inviting college campuses at the University of Utah. Salt Lake City is still the headquarters of the Mormon church and the place to go to see Mormon monuments. But it also has hip restaurants, a budding film scene (a spillover effect from the Sundance Film Festival in nearby Park City), a fresh crop of art galleries and boutiques, and an open-door stance toward refugees and immigrants that has brought a variety of newcomers to town. There's also a new partying spirit in town since Utah liquor laws were normalized in 2009, allowing patrons to simply walk into a bar and order a drink.
— BY JAIME GROSS AND CHRIS DIXON

FRIDAY

1 *Creative Souvenirs* 4 p.m.

With its relatively affordable rents and do-it-yourself ethos, Salt Lake City is a bastion of creativity. To survey the design scene, stop by **Frosty Darling** (177 East Broadway; 801-532-4790; frostydarling.com), a whimsical gift shop stocked with retro candy and handmade clothing, accessories, and house wares by the owner, Gentry Blackburn, and other Utah designers. **Signed & Numbered** (2105 East 2100 South; 801-596-2093; signed-numbered.com) specializes in limited-edition, hand-pulled art prints and concert posters. And at **Salt Lake Citizen** (210 East 400 South; 801-363-3619), in the atrium of the Main Library building, you'll find street-inspired clothing and accessories from 40 city designers. One season's selection included embroidered jeans and jewelry made of laser-cut acrylic.

2 *Utah Farms* 7 p.m.

Chain restaurants used to dominate in Salt Lake City, but today intimate spots are popping up, run by young chefs inspired by the bounty of local organic farmers and artisanal purveyors. **Pago** (878 South 900 East; 801-532-0777; pagoslc.com; $$$), a bustling neighborhood joint housed in a squat 1910 brick building, spotlights local organic products in dishes like steak with heirloom fingerling potatoes and local arugula. The rustic candle-lit dining room seats just 50. **Forage** (370 East 900 South; 801-708-7834; foragerestaurant.com; $$$), serves wildly creative dishes like vanilla-scented diver scallops paired with smoked beluga lentils.

3 *Open City* 9 p.m.

Raise a glass to celebrate the repeal of liquor laws that until 2009 required bars to operate as private clubs and collect membership fees. **The Red Door** (57 West 200 South; 801-363-6030; behindthereddoor.com) has dim lighting, a great martini list and kitschy revolution décor — yes, that's a Che Guevara mural on the wall. **Squatters Pub Brewery** (147 West Broadway; 801-363-2739; squatters.com) serves high-gravity beers from the award-winning brewmaster Jenny Talley, like the 6 percent alcohol India Pale Ale. And **Club Jam** (751 North 300 West; 801-891-1162; jamslc.com) is a friendly gay bar with a house party feel and impromptu barbecues on the back patio.

SATURDAY

4 *Botanical Bliss* 9 a.m.

The **Red Butte Garden**, nestled in the foothills above the University of Utah campus (300 Wakara

OPPOSITE The Salt Lake City Public Library, designed by Moshe Safdie.

BELOW Pago, one in a crop of new restaurants.

Way; 801-585-0556; redbuttegarden.org), has a rose garden, 3.5 miles of walking trails, and morning yoga in the fragrance garden. For a wake-up hike, ask the front desk for directions to the Living Room, a lookout point named for the flat orange rocks that resemble couches. Sit back and absorb the expansive views of the valley, mountains, and the Great Salt Lake.

5 *City Structure* 11 a.m.

Chart your own architecture tour. The city's **Main Library** (210 East 400 South; 801-524-8200; slcpl.lib.ut.us), a curving glass structure built in 2003 and designed by the architect Moshe Safdie, has fireplaces on every floor and a rooftop garden with views of the city and the Wasatch Mountains. For older buildings, wander the **Marmalade Historic District**, home to many original pioneer homes from the 19th century, or go on a walking tour with the **Utah Heritage Foundation** (801-533-0858; utahheritagefoundation.com).

6 *Diverse Palate* 1 p.m.

Salt Lake City has growing contingents of Latinos, Pacific Islanders (particularly Samoan and Tongan), and refugees from Tibet, Bosnia, and Somalia. One place to taste this kind of imported flavor is **Himalayan Kitchen** (360 South State Street; 801-328-2077; himalayankitchen.com; $$), a down-home dining room with turmeric-yellow walls and red tablecloth tables, where you might find Nepali goat curry or Himalayan momos, steamed chicken dumplings served with sesame seed sauce.

7 *Gimme Sugar* 3 p.m.

The **Sugarhouse District** is known for its one-of-a-kind shops and pedestrian-friendly mini-neighborhoods that are near the intersections of 900 East and 900 South (which locals call 9th and 9th), and 1500 East and 1500 South (15th and 15th). Highlights include the **Tea Grotto** (2030 South 900 East; 801-466-8255; teagrotto.com), a funky teahouse that specializes in fair-trade and loose-leaf teas, and

the charming **King's English Bookshop** (1511 South 1500 East; 801-484-9100; kingsenglish.com), a creaky old house filled with books and cozy reading nooks.

8 *Italian Hour* 7 p.m.

Salt Lake City has plenty of appealing Italian restaurants, but the most romantic may be **Fresco Italian Cafe** (1513 South 1500 East; 801-486-1300; frescoitaliancafe.com; $$), an intimate 14-table restaurant tucked off the main drag in a 1920s cottage. The menu is small but spot-on, with simple northern Italian dishes with a twist. The butternut squash ravioli, for example, was served with a splash of reduced apple cider and micro-planed hazelnuts. There's a roaring fire, candlelight, and, in the summer, dining on the brick patio.

9 *Live From Utah* 9 p.m.

As the only sizable city between Denver and Northern California, Salt Lake City gets many touring bands passing through. Hear established and up-and-coming acts at places like the **Urban Lounge** (241 South 500 East; 801-746-0557; theurbanloungeslc.com) and **Kilby Court** (741 South Kilby Court; 801-364-3538; kilbycourt.com). If you want to make your own sweet

ABOVE A light rail trolley system runs through downtown past Temple Square and Mormon monuments.

BELOW The University of Utah's Red Butte Garden and Arboretum has 3.5 miles of walking trails.

music, stop by **Keys on Main** (242 South Main Street; 801-363-3638; keysonmain.com), a piano bar where the audience sings along.

SUNDAY

10 *Voices on High* 9 a.m.

Almost every Sunday morning the 360 volunteer members of the Mormon Tabernacle Choir sing at the **Mormon Tabernacle** in Temple Square (801-240-4150; mormontabernaclechoir.org). The egg-shaped hall, with its 150-foot roof span, is an acoustical marvel (tour guides are fond of dropping a pin on the stage to demonstrate just how well sound carries), and the nearly 12,000-pipe organ is among the largest in the

world. You can join the live audience at the concert broadcast from 9:30 to 10 a.m., but you need to be in your seat by 9:15. Admission is free.

11 *Mormon Central* 10:30 a.m.

You're inside **Temple Square**, Utah's No. 1 tourist attraction, so drop in at one of the visitors' centers (visittemplesquare.com) and then take a look around. If you're not a confirmed Mormon, you won't be allowed inside the main temple, but you can get an idea of the interior by visiting the smaller Assembly Hall, built in 1880 with granite left over from construction of the temple. The square is 35 acres, the epicenter of the Mormon Church, and its monumental scale is a spectacle in itself.

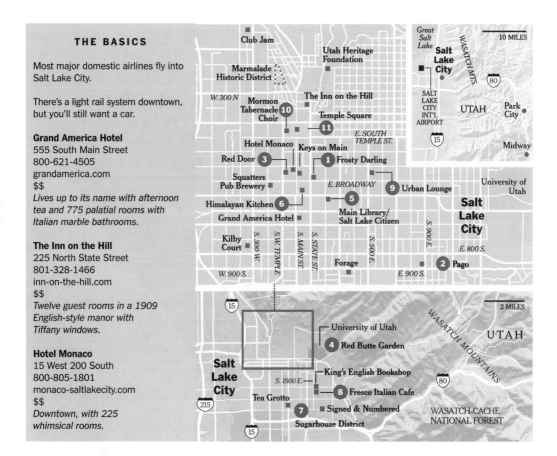

THE BASICS

Most major domestic airlines fly into Salt Lake City.

There's a light rail system downtown, but you'll still want a car.

Grand America Hotel
555 South Main Street
800-621-4505
grandamerica.com
$$
Lives up to its name with afternoon tea and 775 palatial rooms with Italian marble bathrooms.

The Inn on the Hill
225 North State Street
801-328-1466
inn-on-the-hill.com
$$
Twelve guest rooms in a 1909 English-style manor with Tiffany windows.

Hotel Monaco
15 West 200 South
800-805-1801
monaco-saltlakecity.com
$$
Downtown, with 225 whimsical rooms.

Park City

With a year-round population of about 7,500, Park City, Utah, is a small town, but it is far from remote. Downtown trails off quickly and mountains rise up behind it, but those same mountains fill the town with skiers in winter. Main Street is achingly picturesque under a confectioner's sifting of Utah's famous light snow, but it can also be jammed with smoking S.U.V.'s. Over the past few years, thanks to several factors — the 2002 Winter Olympics; the Sundance Film Festival, held here every winter; a growing realization among wealthy skiing baby boomers that this former silver-mining town is "in Utah but not of Utah" — the area boomed with unbridled second-home development near the ski areas. The upside of that change is an infusion of ambitious new hoteliers and chefs in Park City proper, injecting new life and urban sophistication.
— BY CHRISTOPHER SOLOMON

FRIDAY

1 *Stroll the Snowy Strip* 5:30 p.m.

A pleasure of visiting Park City is bundling up as the sky assumes that special mercury light of a winter's twilight in the mountains and walking the four-block historic **Main Street**, with its brightly painted 19th-century storefronts. True, many of the storefronts are filled with ski-town schlock — T-shirts, pricey shards of quartz with contemplative wolves painted on them, and mural-size photo clichés of yellow aspen groves. But the pleasure here is what Italians call la passeggiata: the stroll.

2 *A Gastronomic Empire* 6 p.m.

If Park City has a restaurant empire, it is Bill White Enterprises, which owns several places in town. One of them is the much-recommended **Wahso** (577 Main Street; 435-615-0300; wahso.com; $$$), where the atmosphere suggests Shanghai of the 1930s. For something more in keeping with the Western theme, try White's **Chimayo** (368 Main Street; 435-649-6222; chimayorestaurant.com; $$$),

OPPOSITE For a yank to the adrenal glands, take a turn on the bobsled run at the Utah Olympic Park.

RIGHT Park City's 7,500 residents make room for crowds in ski season and during the Sundance Film Festival.

which serves high-end Southwest fare. There are a dozen kinds of tequila to sample, and you may find elk on the menu, accompanied by a quesadilla.

3 *Hit the Deck* 10 p.m.

Once full of saloons and brothels, Park City doesn't lack for places to kick up your boot heels. The smoke-free, loungelike **Sidecar** (333 Main Street; 435-645-7468; sidecarbar.com) attracts a real mix of patrons who fill the place on weekends to hear live music and enjoy the heated outdoor deck that overlooks Main Street. The place also serves thin-crust pizza from when the lifts close until 1 a.m.

SATURDAY

4 *Wheels Down, Tips Up* 9 a.m.

Most weekend warriors are only starting to realize just how accessible Utah's skiing is. **Park City Mountain Resort**, the **Canyons Resort** (four miles from Park City), and **Deer Valley Resort** (one mile from downtown) are all about a half-hour drive from the Salt Lake City airport, where about 150 flights arrive by noon daily. That means an early-rising flier from the East can be skiing by noon and ambitious Westerners even sooner. Beat the crowd with an early start.

5 *Haute Slopes* 1:30 p.m.

Deer Valley Resort wisely takes a page from European resorts, which know the importance of eating well on the slopes. Reserve a place at the **Royal Street Café** at the midmountain **Silver Lake Lodge** (435-645-6724; deervalley.com; $$), where the usual

uninspired burgers and nachos have been replaced by fare like crayfish bisque, grilled tuna tacos, and roasted game hen-and-shiitake mushroom pot pie. At Park City resort, pop out of your bindings at the base of the town lift and walk to a booth at cherry-paneled **Butcher's Chop House & Bar** (751 Main Street; 435-647-0040; butcherschophouse.com; $$) for polenta-crusted calamari or a half-pound Kobe cheeseburger.

6 *Ski and Shoot* 3 p.m.

Of the many sports that haven't captivated Americans, few baffle like the biathlon, a mixture of Nordic skiing and gunplay. One reason it hasn't been embraced is that there are few places to try it. At **Soldier Hollow** (25 Soldier Hollow Lane, Midway; 435-654-2002; soldierhollow.com), amateurs can try it out. This was the venue for the 2002 Olympics cross-country skiing and biathlon and is about a 25-minute drive south of Park City. No experience is necessary. Programs range from one-hour introductions to

two-hour shooting sessions with air rifles with timed competitions and all-day gear rentals for the groomed trails.

7 *Splashdown* 4:30 p.m.

Scoot five miles north on the way back to Park City to the **Homestead Resort** (700 North Homestead Road, Midway; 800-327-7220; homesteadresort.com), where you can soak in the **Crater**, a 55-foot-tall beehive-shaped limestone rock that nature has filled with Caribbean-blue, 90- to 96-degree mineral water. Even in snow season, it offers swimming, snorkeling, and scuba diving. Reservations are required.

8 *Shrimp and Saketini* 8 p.m.

Shabu (442 Main Street; 435-645-7253; shabupc.com; $$$) exemplifies the changes in Park City. The executive chef and co-owner, Robert Valaika, who opened Nobu Matsuhisa's restaurant in Aspen and studied under Charlie Trotter in Chicago, came to Park City about four years ago hoping to strike out on his own; he opened Shabu with his brother, Kevin. The Asian cuisine — including the Japanese hot pot dish called shabu shabu, is very popular with locals.

9 *Mayoral Bandwagon* 10:30 p.m.

If you haven't left all of your energy on the slopes, take in the **Spur Bar and Grill** (352 Main Street; 435-615-1618; thespurbarandgrill.com). It generally attracts an older crowd (the leather bar chairs and fireplace are one giveaway), but the no-smoking policy means visiting athletes gravitate there, too — not to mention Park City's mayor, Dana Williams, and his Motherlode Canyon Band. Live music on weekends ranges from blues to bluegrass.

SUNDAY

10 *Stoke the Furnace* 9 a.m.

You've got a big day ahead of you and perhaps a hangover to bury after forgetting how quickly alcohol hits you at 7,000 feet. Start it at a Park City institution, the **Eating Establishment** (317 Main Street; 435-649-8284; theeatingestablishment.net; $$), with a tall glass of fresh-squeezed orange juice and a plate of eggs, potatoes, ham, and toast. After this, you can check eating off your to-do list for a while.

11 *Take a Slide* 11 a.m.

For another yank to the adrenal glands, try banging around the inside of a bobsled at 80 miles an hour. For about $200, at the **Utah Olympic Park** (435-658-4200; utaholympiclegacy.com/programs/

comet-bobsled-rides) just outside town, sliders 16 and older can climb behind an experienced driver and run the Olympic bobsled track, including a 40-story drop in just under a minute and up to five G's of force. Reservations are recommended. For younger kids, or for adults who would like much cheaper thrills, try the Alpine Coaster at the main base area of **Park City Mountain Resort** (1345 Lowell Avenue; 435-649-8111; parkcitymountain.com). It's nearly 4,000 feet of bends, bumps, and curves through naked aspens in a toboggan that's secured to a metal track.

OPPOSITE ABOVE Main Street is achingly picturesque but can also be jammed with smoking S.U.V.'s.

OPPOSITE BELOW On the mountain after a confectioner's sifting of Utah's famous light snow.

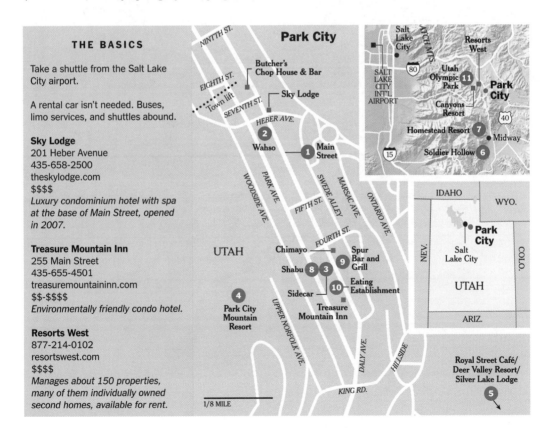

THE BASICS

Take a shuttle from the Salt Lake City airport.

A rental car isn't needed. Buses, limo services, and shuttles abound.

Sky Lodge
201 Heber Avenue
435-658-2500
theskylodge.com
$$$$
Luxury condominium hotel with spa at the base of Main Street, opened in 2007.

Treasure Mountain Inn
255 Main Street
435-655-4501
treasuremountaininn.com
$$-$$$$
Environmentally friendly condo hotel.

Resorts West
877-214-0102
resortswest.com
$$$$
Manages about 150 properties, many of them individually owned second homes, available for rent.

Park City

Butcher's Chop House & Bar
Sky Lodge
Town lift
NINTTH ST.
EIGHTH ST.
SEVENTH ST.
HEBER AVE.
Wahso
Main Street
WOODSIDE AVE.
PARK AVE.
FIFTH ST.
SWEDE ALLEY
MARSAC AVE.
ONTARIO AVE.
UTAH
Chimayo
FOURTH ST.
Spur Bar and Grill
Shabu
Sidecar
Eating Establishment
Park City Mountain Resort
Treasure Mountain Inn
UPPER NORFOLK AVE.
DALY AVE.
HILLSIDE
KING RD.
1/8 MILE

Salt Lake City
Resorts West
SALT LAKE CITY INT'L AIRPORT
Utah Olympic Park
Park City
Canyons Resort
Homestead Resort
Midway
Soldier Hollow
IDAHO
WYO.
Park City
NEV.
Salt Lake City
UTAH
COLO.
ARIZ.
Royal Street Café/ Deer Valley Resort/ Silver Lake Lodge

Boise

Boise, Idaho, once ruled by the bait-and-bullet crowd, has embraced the Lycra lifestyle. Sitting at the junction of the arid plateau of the high desert and the western foothills of the Rocky Mountains, Boise, Idaho's capital, offers all the outdoor advantages of more ballyhooed Western towns but with less, well, ballyhoo. Boise may have a population of more than 200,000, but it is still a mining and farming town at heart, and it attracts active professionals and young families who will tell you that theirs is a great hometown—just don't let too many people know. They wouldn't want those trailheads or hot springs to get too crowded. A rejuvenated downtown and a budding arts community mean that after a day of rafting on the Payette River, mountain biking in the foothills, or carving at Bogus Basin Ski Resort you don't have to turn in once the sun fades behind the Snake River.
— BY MATTHEW PREUSCH

FRIDAY

1 *The Idaho Story* 4 p.m.
It's best to educate before you recreate, so check out the pioneer days reconstructions and Lewis and Clark artifacts at the **Idaho Historical Museum** (610 North Julia Davis Drive; 208-334-2120; history.idaho.gov/museum.html) in **Julia Davis Park**. From there, walk down the **Boise River Greenbelt** (cityofboise.org), a much-loved and gloriously scenic public corridor of parks and trails snug against the Boise River. It stretches for 23 miles, but you won't be going that far tonight.

2 *Big Game* 7 p.m.
Emerge at the **Cottonwood Grille** (913 West River Street; 208-333-9800; cottonwoodgrille.com; $$) to reward yourself with drinks and dinner. Have a cocktail or a glass of wine on the patio overlooking the river and, of course, cottonwoods. Check out the game menu. This is your chance to try elk sirloin, bison with cabernet sauce, or grilled pheasant. If

you're feeling more conventional, there's always the pasta or Idaho trout.

SATURDAY

3 *Breakfast Builders* 8 a.m.
Put your name on the list at **Goldy's Breakfast Bistro** (108 South Capitol Boulevard; 208-345-4100; goldysbreakfastbistro.com; $$) and stroll two blocks north to the domed Capitol to contemplate the statue of Governor Frank Steunenberg. He was killed in 1905 by a bomb planted near his garden gate; the perpetrators were enraged by his rough handling of labor uprisings in upstate mines. But don't let that assassination ruin your appetite. Return to Goldy's and examine the menu to see which elements of the build-your-own breakfast you'd like to have with your scrambled eggs. Red flannel hash? Black beans? Salmon cake? Blueberry pancake? Be creative.

4 *Bumper Crop* 10 a.m.
Join stroller-pushing Boiseans gathered near the Capitol dome at the **Capital City Public Market** (280 North 8th Street; capitalcitypublicmarket.com). Browse amid the lettuces—not to mention the fruit, flowers, desserts, and art glass—and reflect that Idaho grows more than potatoes.

5 *Basque Brawn* 11 a.m.
A century ago, Basque shepherds tended flocks in the grassy foothills around Boise. Today the mayor and many other prominent Idahoans claim Basque heritage. Learn about aspects of the Basques' culture,

OPPOSITE Rafting on the South Fork of the Payette River north of Boise.

RIGHT Join the Boiseans browsing amid carrots and lettuces near the Capitol dome at the Capital City Public Market.

including their love of a stirring strongman competition, at the **Basque Museum and Cultural Center** (611 Grove Street; 208-343-2671; basquemuseum.com). Don't drop the theme when you leave the museum in search of lunch. Grab a table at **Bar Gernika Basque Pub & Eatery** (202 South Capitol Boulevard; 208-344-2175; bargernika.com; $). The lamb grinder is a safe bet, but for something more spirited, brave the beef tongue in tomato and pepper sauce. Wash it down with Basque cider.

6 *Rapid Transit* 1:30 p.m.

Join the weekend exodus of pickups hauling A.T.V.'s and Subarus bearing bikes as they head over the brown foothills of the Boise Front to outdoor adventure. Drive 45 minutes north to Horseshoe Bend and hook up with **Cascade Raft and Kayaking** (7050 Highway 55; 208-793-2221; cascaderaft.com) for a half-day raft trip through Class III and IV rapids on the Lower South Fork of the Payette River. There's also a milder trip with Class II and III rapids. If even that seems like whiter water than you're up for, stay in town, buy an inner tube, and join lazy locals floating down the relatively placid Boise River for six miles

ABOVE Downtown and the Boise Mountains.

OPPOSITE Hikers, runners, and cyclists share the 130 miles of paths in the Ridge to Rivers trail system.

between **Barber Park** (4049 Eckert Road) and **Ann Morrison Park** (1000 Americana Boulevard). Avoid the river if the water is high.

7 *How about a Potato-tini?* 7 p.m.

Swap your swimsuit for town wear and find an outdoor table on the pedestrian plaza outside the overtly cosmopolitan **Red Feather Lounge** (246 North 8th Street; 208-429-6340; justeatlocal.com/ redfeather; $$), where the focus is on post-classic cocktails, like the Tangerine Rangoon: Plymouth gin, fresh tangerine juice and homemade pomegranate grenadine. Pair that with sockeye salmon or truffled duck egg pizza, and you might forget that you're in laid-back Boise. That is, until you spot the guy in running shorts and a fanny pack sitting at the bar.

8 *Bard by the Boise* 8 p.m.

Borrow a blanket from your hotel and find a spot on the lawn at the **Idaho Shakespeare Festival**, overlooking the Boise River east of town (5657 Warm Springs Avenue; 208-336-9221; idahoshakespeare.org), which runs June to September. It features productions of Shakespeare as well as more contemporary works at an outdoor amphitheater. As the sun sets and the stars come out, you might start to think that Boise's status as one of the most isolated metro areas in the lower 48 states is not a bad thing.

SUNDAY

9 *Pedal for Your Coffee* 9 a.m.

Head to **Idaho Mountain Touring** (1310 West Main Street; 208-336-3854; idahomountaintouring.com), rent a full-suspension mountain bike, and head north on 13th Street to Hyde Park, a neighborhood of bungalows and tree-lined streets. Park your bike with the others in front of **Java Hyde Park** (1612 North 13th Street; 208-345-4777) and make your way past the dogs tied up outside to order your favorite caffeinated creation.

10 *Up, Down, Repeat* 10 a.m.

Fortified, and perhaps jittery, remount your rented ride and pedal a few blocks farther up 13th

Street to **Camel's Back Park** (1200 West Heron Street). Look for the trailhead east of the tennis courts, one of many entrances to the Ridge to Rivers trail system (ridgetorivers.cityofboise.org), a single- and double-track network that covers 80,000 acres between the Boise Ridge and Boise River. Climb the Red Cliffs Trail to open vistas of the Treasure Valley below, then loop back down on the rollicking Lower Hulls Gulch Trail. Repeat as necessary.

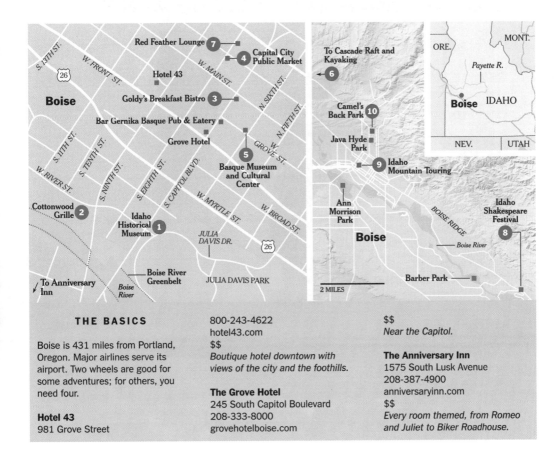

THE BASICS

Boise is 431 miles from Portland, Oregon. Major airlines serve its airport. Two wheels are good for some adventures; for others, you need four.

Hotel 43
981 Grove Street

800-243-4622
hotel43.com
$$
Boutique hotel downtown with views of the city and the foothills.

The Grove Hotel
245 South Capitol Boulevard
208-333-8000
grovehotelboise.com

$$
Near the Capitol.

The Anniversary Inn
1575 South Lusk Avenue
208-387-4900
anniversaryinn.com
$$
Every room themed, from Romeo and Juliet to Biker Roadhouse.

Sun Valley

Nostalgia can feel like the dominant mode at the Sun Valley Resort near Ketchum, Idaho, which was founded by W. Averell Harriman in 1936 to bring passengers to the West on the Union Pacific Railroad. Just check out the photographs in the hallways at the Sun Valley Lodge — isn't that Gary Cooper, Janet Leigh, Lucille Ball? All were high-glam-quotient visitors to this resort during its Hollywood glory days. Ernest Hemingway was also a Ketchum regular, and bought his own local ranch. These days you're likely to mingle with less-photogenic tech moguls and their pals, but the guest rooms are updated along with the clientele, and so are the slopes. At Bald Mountain, the bigger of Sun Valley's two ski areas, the Roundhouse gondola has enhanced the experience. At Dollar Mountain, the terrain parks have new rails and jibs. Some things haven't changed. It's a short hop from the resort hotels to the slopes, and "Sun Valley Serenade" still plays, free, on guest room TVs. — BY AMY VIRSHUP

FRIDAY

1 *Skate under the Lights* 6 p.m.

Make like Michelle Kwan and hit the ice at the **Sun Valley Lodge**'s outdoor rink (208-622-2194). This oval has seen performances by all manner of Olympic gold medalists, from Peggy Fleming to Evan Lysacek. So lace up a pair of rental skates and practice your triple lutz. (If your tastes run more to Alex Ovechkin, there are hockey skates available, too.) And if you hear Scott Hamilton doing the commentary in your head, well, you won't be the first — or last. The evening session ends at 8.

2 *Slow Cooker* 8 p.m.

The wood-frame cottage that's home to the **Ketchum Grill** (520 East Avenue North; 208-726-4660; ketchumgrill.com; $$) dates back to Ketchum's first boom industry — silver mining, which briefly fueled development here in the 1880s. There are lots of old-fashioned touches at this cozy, cheerful place:

OPPOSITE A snowboarder waits to start a run at the Sun Valley Ski Resort in Ketchum, Idaho.

RIGHT Looking down at the town of Ketchum, where skiers from Sun Valley descend to find all sorts of sustenance.

the oversize rodeo poster as you walk in, the kayak suspended overhead in the back dining room, the rustic apple tart with homemade ice cream on the dessert menu. But the owners Scott Mason, chef, and his wife, Anne, pastry chef, are up on the latest trends. There's always a "slow cooked food of the day" entree: stuffed pork loin, short ribs or maybe house-cured corned beef with cabbage and boiled potatoes. And the steak of the day might come with pomegranate sauce, gorgonzola butter, or mushrooms.

SATURDAY

3 *Breakfast with a View* 8:30 a.m.

The slopes don't officially open until 9, but you can get an early start by riding the gondola to the **Roundhouse** for breakfast (about $15 for those with lift tickets; $30 for those without). Perched 7,700 feet up Baldy, the Roundhouse was the first day lodge on the mountain, and its exposed rafters, four-sided fireplace and antler chandeliers feel as if they've barely changed since it opened in 1939. The breakfast is continental — fruit, Danish, artisan breads, juices, and coffee — and the views are striking. A good number of your fellow diners may have really worked up an appetite, as it's a popular stop for skiers who have walked up the mountain with climbing skins on their boards. If you time things right, you can be first in line at the **Christmas chair** lift when it opens.

4 *Hit the Slopes* 9 a.m.

Some mountains require elaborate strategizing to avoid the lift lines, but at Sun Valley that's rarely

a problem. What does take some thought is working around Bald Mountain's relatively low elevation, which means that the lower half of the mountain can get slushy in the afternoon sun and then freeze overnight. So start your morning up high at the **Seattle Ridge** area. The slopes up here, named for Sun Valley's Olympic stars and their medals—Gretchen's Gold, Christin's Silver—are mostly greens, but their consistent pitch down the fall line makes them eminently swooshable on morning legs. Once you've warmed up, Christmas Bowl, from the top of the Christmas chair, is the longest run on the mountain, starting out as a blue and then turning into an expert run down below. Feel ready? The **Mayday chair** takes you up to the Easter, Lookout, and Mayday bowls. If you feel overwhelmed, keep going left to the easier Broadway Face or Sigi's Bowl.

5 *Refresh Your Look* 4 p.m.

If your skiwear needs a little sprucing up, knock off early and head to the **Gold Mine Thrift Store** (331 Walnut Avenue, Ketchum; 208-726-3465), where

ABOVE Skis as fencing: themed architecture along the road between the Sun Valley resort and Ketchum.

BELOW Downhill is not the only kind of skiing around Sun Valley. Extensive networks of cross-country trails wind through the countryside.

the used stock runs heavily to the brand-name and all but brand-new. Among the finds: a men's Giorgio Armani jumpsuit for $75; numerous Bogner parkas and ski pants for women for about $80 each; and enough children's Obermeyer bibs to outfit a ski school, plus Burton snowboards, skis from K2, Rossignol, and Salomon, and vintage ski sweaters. Proceeds benefit the Community Library. Around the corner, **Iconoclast Books** (671 Sun Valley Road, Ketchum; 208-726-1564; iconoclastbooks.com) has current adult and children's books, but its real strength is its Hemingway-related collection, including selected first editions of many of his novels plus biographies and memoirs by far-flung members of the clan. Or discover other Idaho writers, like Vardis Fisher, whose 1965 novel *Mountain Man* was the basis for the film *Jeremiah Johnson*, with Robert Redford.

6 *Cross-Cultural Eating* 8 p.m.

Derek Gallegos, the chef and owner of **310 Main** in Ketchum's scruffier neighbor, Hailey, grew up in the restaurant business. His family owned an Idaho chain of Mexican places called Mama Inez; later he worked in Deer Valley, Utah, and at the Sun Valley Brewing Company. In this tidy 35-seat spot on Hailey's main drag (310 North Main, Hailey; 208-788-4161; threetenmain.com; $$), Gallegos mashes up his influences to create starters like Shanghai Tacos or Homa Homa oysters with habanero and lime sorbet. And there's always the rib-eye steak with mashed potatoes. You're in Idaho, after all.

7 *Drink with the Wildlife* 10 p.m.

Back in Ketchum, the **Pioneer Saloon** (320 North Main Street; 208-726-3139) is probably as famous for its décor as it is for its food. There's taxidermy galore—heads of deer (the one over the dining room entrance is named Fred and was shot in 1927), elk, and bison; stuffed grouse and pheasant; and even trophy trout (the enormous one is actually a fiberglass replica of a record steelhead). That's not to mention the birch-bark canoe hanging in the bar, or the numerous bullet and rifle displays. Admire them all while having one of the Pioneer's signature bartender margaritas or a draft Sun Valley ale at the bar.

SUNDAY

8 *Brunch by the Fire* 9 a.m.

Tucked away on a side street but worth finding, **Cristina's** (520 Second Street East; 208-726-4499; cristinasofsunvalley.com; $$) is a Sun Valley institution. It serves homey food in a trim salmon-pink cottage where a fire burns all winter long in the fireplace. The Sunday brunch menu mixes classic breakfast fare like French toast and omelets with items like 10-inch thin-crust pizzas. The breads are homemade — prune walnut is a house specialty.

9 *Time for Skinny Skis* 10 a.m.

Downhill is not the only kind of skiing in Sun Valley. There are extensive networks of cross-country trails that wind through the countryside. Get outfitted at the **Elephant's Perch** (280 East Avenue; 208-726-3497; elephantsperch.com), where a touring package rents for about $15 for a half day. (You'll also need a day pass for the trails, which costs about the same.) Head north and pick up the Harriman Trail near the Sawtooth National Recreation Area headquarters (seven miles north of Ketchum on Route 75). It's gentle and flat and runs along the banks of the Big Wood River. Farther north you can try the Prairie Creek Loop, with views of the Boulder and Smoky Mountains. For trail information, check with the Blaine County Recreation District (208-578-9754; bcrd.org).

THE BASICS

Fly into Boise and rent a car or use the Sun Valley Express Shuttle for the two-and-a-half-hour drive to Sun Valley. In town, the Mountain Fairy (208-720-0776; mtnfairy.blogspot.com) offers rides to outdoor-sports locations.

The Sun Valley Resort
800-786-8259
sunvalley.com
$$$
The biggest game in town, with a lodge and inn, cottages, apartments, and condos.

Knob Hill Inn
960 North Main Street, Ketchum
208-726-8010
knobhillinn.com
$$$-$$$$
High-end rooms and good views.

Best Western Tyrolean Lodge
260 Cottonwood Street, Ketchum
208-726-5336
bestwesternidaho.com
$$
A less expensive alternative.

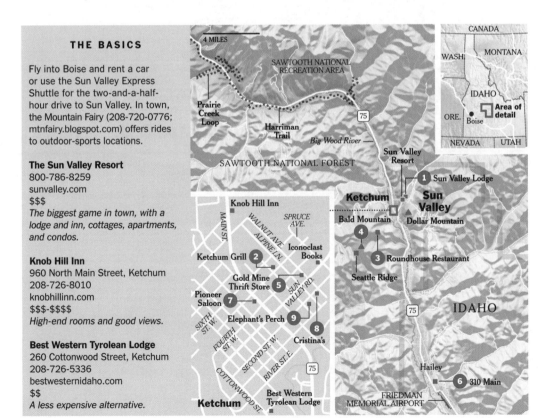

Jackson

At the edge of Grand Teton National Park, among other natural wonders, Jackson, Wyoming (often confused with the wider valley in which it rests, Jackson Hole) has avoided becoming a sprawling tourist trap thanks to its quirk of geography: hemmed in by public land, the town has no room to expand. And the new money drawn here has added cosmopolitan flair without loss of respect for the town's Old West tradition. Sometimes it seems as if you're as likely to see a Buddhist prayer flag as a pickup truck. Add an ever-expanding list of adventure sports, and you've got a destination that packs in enough adrenaline, scenery, and culture per square mile to keep anyone coming back. — BY TOM PRICE

FRIDAY

1 *Western Style* 6 p.m.

Get oriented with a ramble around the town square, which is framed by four arches made from elk horns gathered in nearby forests. Duck into the **Million Dollar Cowboy Bar** (25 North Cache Street; 307-733-2207; milliondollarcowboybar.com) to look over the spur collection and 70 years' worth of other accumulated Westernalia. Then check out some of the nearby shops. **Terra Jackson Hole** (105 East Broadway; 307-734-0067; terrajh.com) stocks designer clothes for women, including strapless dresses, glittery tops, and plenty of denim. For something completely different, walk down the street to **Stone's Mercantile** (50 West Broadway; 307-733-3392; stonesboots.com) for Western boots and hats, motorcycle chaps, and gun belts.

2 *Night Sights* 8 p.m.

Climb the steps to the **Snake River Grill** (84 East Broadway; 307-733-0557; snakerivergrill.com; $$$) and settle down at one of the tables in the log-walled dining room. It's one of Jackson's best-known restaurants — reservations are recommended — and the menu is kept dynamic while maintaining worthy

OPPOSITE Fishing the Snake River. Jackson attracts a well-to-do crowd that loves getting outdoors.

RIGHT Open land just outside of town. Nearby is publicly owned wilderness including Grand Teton National Park.

traditions. Expect dishes like crispy pork shank with orzo, salsa verde, and tomato jam. After dinner, stroll north, toward the **National Elk Refuge**, which abuts town. If the season is right, you may find southbound geese asleep on the grass roof of the visitors center (532 North Cache Street; 307-733-9212; fws.gov/nationalelkrefuge). But look up higher. Away from the lights and neon, you'll have a striking view of the night sky.

SATURDAY

3 *And Wear a Helmet* 9 a.m.

Get fitted for a mountain bike rental at **Hoback Sports** (520 West Broadway; 307-733-5335; hobacksports.com), buy a trail map, and start pedaling. Ride east toward the 20-mile Cache Creek-Game Creek loop through the **Bridger Teton National Forest**. Take either the smooth dirt road or the parallel single-track Putt-Putt Trail, winding along a shaded stream. At the Game Creek turnoff, crank up a short steep climb, and you'll be rewarded with a five-mile descent down sage- and aspen-covered hills before connecting with a paved path back to town.

4 *Picnic with the Tetons* Noon

For all its worldliness, Jackson is a tiny town of about 9,000 full-time residents. Grab picnic fixings at **Backcountry Provisions** (50 West Deloney Street;

307-734-9420; backcountryprovisions.com) and then get a side order of scenery at **Snow King Resort** (corner of Snow King Avenue and King Street; 307-733-5200; snowking.com), the in-town ski area. Hike the piney switchbacks 1.8 miles and 1,571 vertical feet to the summit (45 minutes if you're huffing, but remember you're starting at 6,200 feet). The view stretches 50 miles to Yellowstone, and it's the best place in the valley to see both the town and the Tetons.

5 *Drive-By Shooting* 2:30 p.m.

Relax with a behind-the-wheel wander through **Grand Teton National Park** (307-739-3300; nps.gov/grte). Best bet for scenic photos: loop north on Route 191 past the Snake River Overlook, where you can frame the river that carved the valley and the mountains behind it in one shot. Then head south along Teton Park Road past Jenny Lake. On your way back, stop at **Dornan's** in the town of Moose (200 Moose Street; 307-733-2415; dornans.com) for cocktails on the deck, about as close as you can get to the Tetons and still have someone bring you a drink.

6 *Japanese Plus* 7 p.m.

At **the Kitchen** (155 North Glenwood Street; 307-734-1633; kitchenjacksonhole.com; $$$), a Japanese bistro in a casual, contemporary space, you can start with truffle fries or sashimi and move on to veal in a chile-miso broth or an organic burger. The drinks menu has similar mixed influences. There's a wide selection of sakes and 19 different types of tequila.

7 *Moose Music* 10 p.m.

Drive the 12 miles to Teton Village to join the locals crowding into the **Mangy Moose Restaurant and Saloon** (Teton Village, Village Road; 307-733-4913; mangymoose.net), where the live music includes national and local acts. Order a draft beer and elbow into a seat at the bar—no matter who's playing.

SUNDAY

8 *Never Toasted* 7:30 a.m.

Join the lineup for coffee at **Pearl Street Bagels** (145 West Pearl Avenue; 307-739-1218). Purists, rejoice; even after pranksters nailed a dozen toasters to Pearl Street's pink facade several years ago, it still serves its bagels warm from the oven but always untoasted. And with bagels this fresh and good, it seems a little unfair to quibble.

9 *Big Red Box* 9 a.m.

If the caffeine didn't get you going, this ride will. From the Teton Village base, the **Jackson Hole Mountain Resort tram** (tram-formation.com) will whisk you up 4,139 feet to the summit of Rendezvous Mountain. (Pack a jacket—it can be gorgeous in

the valley but snowing up top.) Coming down, press against the front window for a stomach-dropping pass over the skier's jump known as Corbet's Couloir. There's been a "big red box" on this mountain since 1966, but the beloved original was retired and replaced by this newer, larger, more streamlined version in 2008. The new version holds 100 people, twice the old one's capacity. But the view is still spectacular.

10 *The Compleat Angler* 10 a.m.

Not every full-service hotel is likely to have a director of fishing, but this is Jackson Hole, and you'll find one at the **Four Seasons Resort** (7680 Granite Loop Road, Teton Village; 307-732-5000; fourseasons.com/jacksonhole). In the resort's

handmade wooden dory, he'll take you down one of the secluded braids of the Snake River and offer expert advice on how to reel in some of the Snake's 2,500 fish per mile. You don't have to be a guest, even first-timers are welcome, and it's safe to feel very surprised if you don't land a fish. A day trip will set you back several hundred dollars, and if it's a couple of hundred too many, you can look for a less expensive guide back in town.

OPPOSITE ABOVE The Westernalia on display at the Million Dollar Cowboy Bar includes a collection of spurs.

OPPOSITE BELOW Arches downtown are made from antlers, a material the local elk obligingly shed each spring.

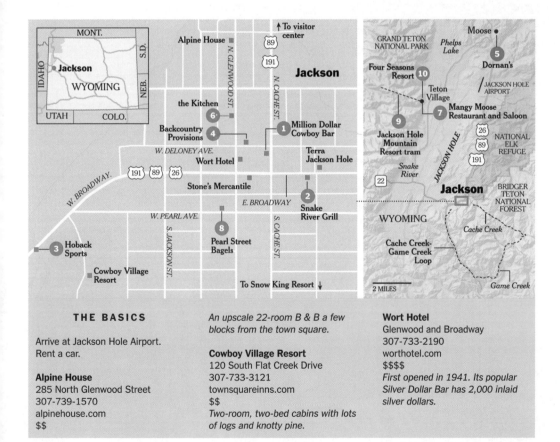

THE BASICS

Arrive at Jackson Hole Airport. Rent a car.

Alpine House
285 North Glenwood Street
307-739-1570
alpinehouse.com
$$

An upscale 22-room B & B a few blocks from the town square.

Cowboy Village Resort
120 South Flat Creek Drive
307-733-3121
townsquareinns.com
$$
Two-room, two-bed cabins with lots of logs and knotty pine.

Wort Hotel
Glenwood and Broadway
307-733-2190
worthotel.com
$$$$
First opened in 1941. Its popular Silver Dollar Bar has 2,000 inlaid silver dollars.

Denver

Denver, Colorado, is a city in a constant state of reinvention, having, in the last decade alone, greatly expanded its cultural institutions, asserted itself in the political discourse by hosting the 2008 Democratic convention, and—despite the challenge presented to chefs by its elevation—embraced a new foodie culture. It was no small point of pride for the energized Mile High City that its increasingly diverse population has been growing, reversing an exodus of families to the suburbs. Visiting some of its recently refurbished attractions, especially the now bustling LoDo district, it's hard to escape the feeling of a modern gold rush.
— BY ERIC WILSON

FRIDAY

1 *Vertical Mile* 1 p.m.

Walk across Civic Center Park to the steps of the imposingly gray state **Capitol**, a dead ringer for the one in Washington except that it's a study in Colorado granite instead of white marble. Ascend the west side to find the spot, around the 13th step, that is exactly 5,280 feet above sea level. The gold marker makes it official: Denver deserves its altitudinal nickname.

2 *Change to Believe In* 2 p.m.

Remember those pennies imprinted with a "D" that you found in your childhood coin-collecting phase? Now is your chance to visit the **Denver Mint** (320 West Colfax Avenue; 303-405-4761; usmint.gov) and see where they came from. You'll get some history along with an explanation of how coins are made, but won't see much of the actual production. Reservations are highly recommended (usmint.gov/mint_tours). Just about everything in your pockets is forbidden, so dress as you would for the airport.

3 *The Urban Outdoors* 4 p.m.

Coloradans are passionate about the outdoors, even in the city. Denver has more than 100 miles of pedestrian and bicycle paths, and you can get to one of the most popular, the **Cherry Creek Path**, right downtown. Hop on the MallRide, a free bus service along 16th Street, at the Civic Center. Hop off at Larimer Street and walk a couple of blocks southwest on Larimer to find the steps down to the creek level. Take the path north, staying alert for

occasional glimpses of the snow-capped Rockies, and arrive at **Confluence Park**, where the creek meets the South Platte River. This is the historic center of Denver, the spot where the city had its start. Continue on the path until you've had enough, and then return.

4 *Where's the Beef?* 7 p.m.

There's no getting around Denver's culinary specialty, red meat, the starring attraction at Old West-themed grill joints all over town. Count the Wild West species represented in the form of taxidermy on the walls (or on the menu) of **Buckhorn Exchange**, billed as Denver's oldest restaurant (1000 Osage Street; 303-534-9505; buckhornexchange.com; $$$). Here, steak can be ordered by the pound. Another option is to drive to the **Fort**, 18 miles southwest in Morrison (19192 Highway 8; 303-697-4771; thefort.com; $$$), where 80,000 buffalo entrees are served annually in what appears to be a 1960s rendition of the Alamo. The food and service may be as wooden as the décor, but seldom is heard a discouraging word, as the music is turned up real loud.

SATURDAY

5 *The Old Glass Ceiling* 10 a.m.

One of Denver's most famous homes belonged to a backwoods social climber who set out in the 1880s

OPPOSITE The Denver Art Museum's new Hamilton building, designed by Daniel Libeskind.

BELOW Dining at Rioja in Larimer Square, near where gold was first discovered in Colorado in the 1850s.

to land herself a rich husband and a big house on what was then called Pennsylvania Avenue. (Now it's Pennsylvania Street.) Margaret Tobin Brown, later mythologized as Molly Brown, was a suffragette who survived the sinking of the *Titanic* and ran for United States Senate, unsuccessfully, years before women won the right to vote. Certain spurned trailblazers might find solace in a tour of her Victorian mansion (**Molly Brown House Museum**, 1340 Pennsylvania Street; 303-832-4092; mollybrown.org). They might even be inspired to stand on the front porch like Debbie Reynolds in the 1964 *The Unsinkable Molly Brown* and holler, "Pennsylvania Avenue, I'll admit you gave me a nose full of splinters, but it's all good wood from the very best doors!"

6 *Meet the Artist* 1 p.m.

Denver has a wealth of remarkable galleries, concentrated in Lower Downtown (LoDo) and also along Santa Fe Drive. For novices, one of the most accessible is **Artists on Santa Fe** (747 Santa Fe Drive; 303-573-5903; artistsonsantafe.com), a warren of studios where sculptors and painters in residence will personally explain their work. Wander down the street and you'll find many more.

7 *How the West Was Worn* 4 p.m.

Let's say you have an image problem. Some people, misguided as they may be, think you are an elitist. Now, that's nothing that can't be fixed with a little fashion makeover at **Rockmount Ranch Wear** (1626 Wazee Street; 303-629-7777; rockmount.com), a LoDo shop famous in these parts for introducing the snap button to the western shirt, making it easier

ABOVE The Victorian trophy home of the "unsinkable" *Titanic* survivor, Molly Brown.

RIGHT Dead animals on the walls and red meat on the plate — that's the Buckhorn Exchange, Denver's oldest restaurant.

OPPOSITE The gallery strip on Denver's Santa Fe Drive.

for cowboys to ride the range or re-enact scenes from *Brokeback Mountain*. (Yep, Jack and Ennis were Rockmount customers.) The store — and an accompanying museum — have the fascinating feel of a ghost town relic, with a lasso-rope logo and dusty displays, but the shirts have modern-day prices.

8 *All That Glitters* 8 p.m.

The best of Denver night life can be found in LoDo, around where gold was first discovered in Colorado in the 1850s. Now the closest thing to gold around here is more likely to come in a bottle of Cuervo. At **Rioja**, for example, you can precede your pasta or grilled salmon dinner with the likes of the Loca Hot, made with Fresno pepper-infused tequila, plus Agavero (tequila liqueur), orange, and lime (1431 Larimer Street; 303-820-2282; riojadenver.com; $$-$$$). It's a short walk from here to a wine bar, Crú, and a Champagne bar, Corridor 44. Given the intensified effects of alcohol at high altitudes, you might want to head underground to **Lannie's Clocktower Cabaret**, the local singer Lannie Garrett's place in the basement of the D&F Tower (16th Street and Arapahoe Street; 303-293-0075; lannies.com). Be warned: the raunchy burlesque shows late on Saturday nights may involve some sort of spanking or drag acts.

SUNDAY

9 *Juxtapositions* 10 a.m.

The **Denver Art Museum**'s jutting addition, designed by Daniel Libeskind, looks like an Imperial

Cruiser from *Star Wars*, and once you are inside, the vertigo-inducing floor plan will make you long to get your feet back on earth (100 West 14th Avenue; 720-865-5000; denverartmuseum.org). But the museum's juxtaposition of the work of contemporary art stars with American Indian artifacts is oddly compelling. And if you happen to be having trouble giving up smoking, be sure to look for Damien Hirst's *Party Time* installation, an ashtray the size of a kiddie pool filled with thousands of burned cigarette butts. Dive right in.

10 *Horizontal Mile* 1 p.m.

The **Mile High Flea Market** could just as well be named the Mile Wide Flea Market, given that its hundreds of tightly packed, pastel-colored stalls cover 80 acres of pavement (I-76 and 88th Avenue; milehighmarketplace.com). Browse through T-shirts, watermelons, antiques, fishing tackle, jewelry, and as many other kinds of merchandise as you can take. You can also sample delicious street fare, like corn on the cob rolled in a tray of butter, Parmesan, and seasoning salt. And if you're man enough, try a chelada, a stomach-churning brew of Clamato juice and Budweiser.

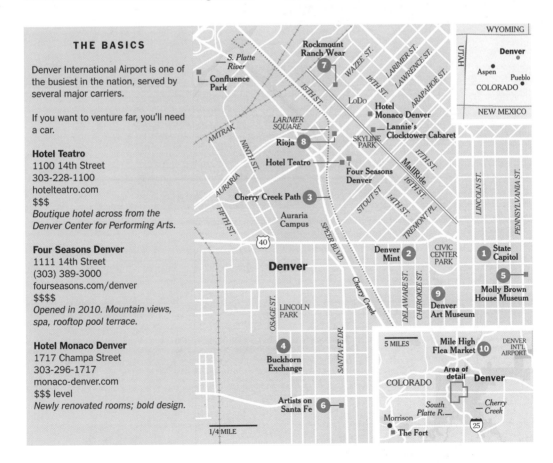

THE BASICS

Denver International Airport is one of the busiest in the nation, served by several major carriers.

If you want to venture far, you'll need a car.

Hotel Teatro
1100 14th Street
303-228-1100
hotelteatro.com
$$$
Boutique hotel across from the Denver Center for Performing Arts.

Four Seasons Denver
1111 14th Street
(303) 389-3000
fourseasons.com/denver
$$$$
Opened in 2010. Mountain views, spa, rooftop pool terrace.

Hotel Monaco Denver
1717 Champa Street
303-296-1717
monaco-denver.com
$$$ level
Newly renovated rooms; bold design.

Leadville

Leadville, Colorado, is a rugged mining town perched at a lung-searing 10,152 feet. Victorian buildings cram Harrison Avenue, the main street in its 70-block historic district. Gold and silver made this a boomtown in the 1800s; a molybdenum mine operated until the 1980s. When the mineral-based economy collapsed, Leadville persevered by retooling itself as a tourist destination. Today mountain bikers and horseback riders hit the trails, and anglers pull rainbows from high mountain lakes. Intrepid hikers scale Mounts Elbert and Massive, the 14,000-foot peaks that dominate the skyline. But most tourists are drawn simply by the Western authenticity that gives the place a unique charm. "Leadville's got character," said Chris Albers, a transplant from South Dakota who owns a bicycle store and a coffee shop in town. "It's not just another slick pop-up ski town." — BY HELEN OLSSON

FRIDAY

1 *Streets of Gold* 4 p.m.

Pick up maps for walking and driving tours at the **Leadville Chamber of Commerce** (809 Harrison Avenue; 888-532-3845; leadvilleusa.com), and set out to get acquainted. The walking tour guides you around Harrison Avenue, where the legacy of the golden era can still be seen. Start at the Tabor Opera House, built in 1879 by Horace Tabor, a silver magnate. Climb onto the stage where Oscar Wilde once performed — and where live horses galloped on a treadmill during a production of *Ben-Hur*. Another stop is Western Hardware, now an antiques store jam-packed with relics and replicas, including brothel tokens for $3 apiece. Wander off the tour route onto the town's back alleys and side streets, which are peppered with sagging outhouses, boarded-up barns, and half-painted churches with broken stained glass windows.

2 *Pasta Pig-Out* 6 p.m.

Linger over a glass of Bolla Valpolicella at **Zichittella's** (422 Harrison Avenue; 719-486-1298; $$). While you wait for homemade meatballs simmered in marinara, gaze at the trompe l'oeil ceiling of clouds above. A rooster, the restaurant's icon, is hidden in the cumulonimbus. Near the bar, Plexiglass covers the 12-foot deep, brick-lined cistern built in 1879. Italian lessons are piped into the bathrooms so you can learn handy phrases like, "Ho capelli ricci," which means, "I have curly hair."

3 *Down at the Saloon* 8 p.m.

Post tiramisu, head across the street to the **Silver Dollar Saloon** (315 Harrison Avenue; 719-486-9914) for a Budweiser longneck. Before you duck in, look up at the building's intricate bracketed cornice, painted green and yellow. Inside, slide into a booth or shoot pool on the 1930s pool table while listening to Johnny Cash on the juke box. Belly up next to locals in jeans and cowboy hats in the original Brunswick back bar, which has diamond dust mirrors and ornately carved columns of white oak.

SATURDAY

4 *Coffee Couch* 8:30 a.m.

Stop in at **Provin' Grounds Coffee & Bakery** (508 Harrison Avenue; 719-486-0797), Chris Albers's hip coffee shop, located in yet another historic building, this one a brick Victorian painted bright green. Plop onto the couch next to locals sipping lattes and pecking on laptops. Have your cup of Joe with a blueberry crisp or buttermilk scone made from scratch.

5 *The Stone You Chew* 9 a.m.

At the **National Mining Hall of Fame and Museum** (120 West Ninth Street; 719-486-1229;

OPPOSITE Old mining shacks, a Leadville legacy.

BELOW Old West antiques pack Western Hardware on Harrison Avenue. One interesting find was brothel tokens.

mininghalloffame.org), marvel at a model of the ice castle Leadville constructed out of 5,000 tons of ice in 1896. For rockhounds, there's a 2,155-pound hunk of galena, icelike logs of selenite, chunks of polished malachite. Here you will learn that the sparkle in your eye shadow comes from mica and the dust on your chewing gum is limestone.

6 *Ballad of Baby Doe* 10:30 a.m.

During the brutal winter of 1935, Baby Doe Tabor, the second wife of Horace Tabor, was found frozen to death in the cabin at the **Matchless Mine** (East 7th Street; 719-486-1229; matchlessmine.com), where she had lived as a recluse for 35 years. Tour the mine and hear their riches-to-rags story. She was a bodacious, round-eyed beauty; he was a silver magnate who spent lavishly: a $90,000 diamond necklace; diamond-studded diaper pins; 100 peacocks to strut on their mansion grounds in Denver. When the price of silver crashed in 1893, they were left penniless. Alongside the cabin are the mining buildings that once produced the millions.

7 *Thin-Air Pizza* 12:30 p.m.

Tucked on a side street, in an 1800s log cabin painted royal blue, purple, green, and red, **High Mountain Pies** (115 West 4th Street; 719-486-5555; $$) serves up pizzas, calzones, and subs. Slinging dough behind the bar is Dru Pashley, 28, a wiry runner who can tell you about the notorious Leadville 100—every summer, he joins the other ultramarathoners running 100 miles of rocky trail in the thin air. (T-shirts for sale in Leadville riff on the milk campaign: "Got Oxygen?")

8 *Ride the Rails* 2 p.m.

Rumble on a scenic passenger train along the old South Park rails, where freight cars once hauled ore from the Climax mine. The **Leadville, Colorado & Southern** passenger train (326 East Seventh Street; 866-386-3936; leadville-train.com) runs trips twice daily in summer. The train starts in downtown Leadville and follows the headwaters of the Arkansas River as it meanders through fields of sagebrush. It chugs toward the Continental Divide through aspen and lodgepole forests and past old mining structures. In July and August, there are special tours for viewing wildflowers.

9 *Head for the Hills* 5 p.m.

The best way to appreciate Leadville's mining pedigree is to explore the mining district firsthand. Walk, or jog, on the 11.6-mile **Mineral Belt Trail** (mineralbelttrail.com), a paved path that circum-navigates Leadville and its adjacent mining district. Bikers, inline skaters, and skateboarders use the trail, rolling by a landscape dotted with rusting ore carts, slumping wooden shacks, and old head frames and hoists. Next to a tailings pond filled with water the color of boiled beets, a superfluous sign warns, "No Swimming."

10 *Margarita with a View* 7 p.m.

Leave Harrison Street behind for the **Grill** (715 Elm Street; 719-486-9930; grillbarcafe.com), a family-owned New Mexican-style Mexican restaurant in a

ABOVE Peaks above town rise to 14,000 feet.

BELOW Twin Lakes, a former stagecoach stop, is the gateway to the ruins of the once-glittering Interlaken resort.

peachy-pink stucco building at the outskirts of town. Every fall, ten tons of Anaheim chiles from Pueblo, Colorado, are harvested and fire-roasted for the Grill's kitchen. Sit on the patio and enjoy the gardens and the mountain views. The chicken sopapillas are enormous, and the house margaritas are served by the liter.

SUNDAY

11 *Ghost Resort* 11 a.m.

Drive south from Leadville 20 miles to the tiny town of Twin Lakes. An 1879 stagecoach stop and brothel for miners heading over Independence Pass to Aspen, it's now a ramshackle collection of dirt roads,

sloping 1800s shacks, and log cabins. Columbines grow among the weeds. Rent a boat at **Twin Lakes Canoe & Kayak** (719-251-9961; coloradovacation.com/outdoors/twinlakerentals). The outfit is run by Johnny Gwaltney, a k a Johnny Canoe, who wears purple-tinted glasses and a giant silver belt buckle, and calls himself a "hikerneck" — a cross between a hippie, a biker, and a redneck. Paddle half an hour across Twin Lakes to the abandoned Interlaken resort, where Denver's upper crust vacationed in the 1880s. Of the handful of buildings, including a hexagonal six-stall privy that once featured leather seats, only Dexter Cabin has been restored. Inside, explore rooms decorated in eight different imported woods and climb a steep ladder to a cupola overlooking the lake.

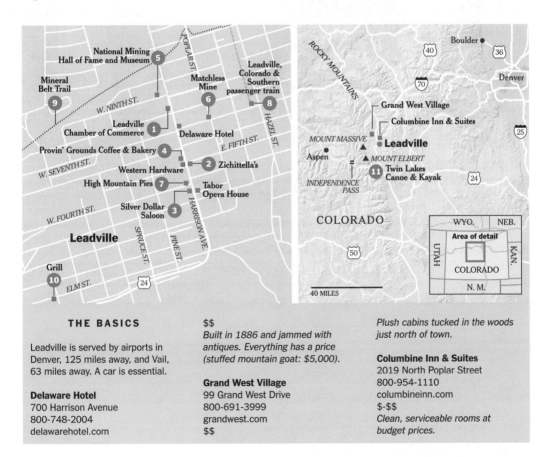

THE BASICS

Leadville is served by airports in Denver, 125 miles away, and Vail, 63 miles away. A car is essential.

Delaware Hotel
700 Harrison Avenue
800-748-2004
delawarehotel.com

$$
Built in 1886 and jammed with antiques. Everything has a price (stuffed mountain goat: $5,000).

Grand West Village
99 Grand West Drive
800-691-3999
grandwest.com
$$

Plush cabins tucked in the woods just north of town.

Columbine Inn & Suites
2019 North Poplar Street
800-954-1110
columbineinn.com
$-$$
Clean, serviceable rooms at budget prices.

Vail

Vail is not the most glamorous of Colorado's ski towns. It does not have the charm of Telluride. Nor does it exude the glitz of Aspen. Even Breckenridge, arguably, has better night life. But the one thing that Vail does have is great snow: some 5,300 skiable acres with a seven-mile-long mountain face, 193 trails, and not one but seven bowls. That hasn't stopped Vail, the United States' largest ski resort by area, from polishing its base village. As part of an upgrade, many of Vail's boxy, 1970s-style facades and outdated streetscapes have been refreshed in the past few years with a modern Bavarian look. Skiers now check into new boutique hotels with ski valets, get pine-scented massages at Zen-channeling spas, and warm themselves by outdoor fire pits.
— BY ELAINE GLUSAC

FRIDAY

1 *Nordic at Dusk* 3:30 p.m.

You don't need to be on the slopes to appreciate the Southern Rockies, 10,000-plus-foot-tall peaks that edge narrow Vail Valley, cut by clear mountain streams that flow in winter's deep freeze. While it's still daylight, explore this winter wonderland on cross-country skis. At the **Vail Nordic Center** (1778 Vail Valley Drive; 970-476-8366; vailnordiccenter.com), trails loop across wooden bridges, gentle pine stands, and snow-blanketed golf fairways.

2 *Western Chic* 5:30 p.m.

Like the mountainside chalets that share a modern rustic look — beamed ceilings, cathedral windows, stone decks — so, too, does the local fashion, which could be described as upscale cowboy. Get into the spirit at **Gorsuch** (263 East Gore Creek Drive; 970-476-2294; gorsuch.com), a luxe store with von Trapp-gone-Vail looks for her (crystal-studded cashmere hats), him (Johann Gottfried suede jackets), and home (Megeve crystal-etched wineglasses). Nearby is **Axel's** (201 Gore Creek Drive; 970-476-7625; axelsltd.com), which carries British tweed sportcoats, shearling coats, and oversized etched belt buckles.

OPPOSITE Après-ski afterglow in Vail.

RIGHT Known for its abundant snow, Vail has 5,300 skiable acres as well as space for pursuits like snowshoeing.

For that rugged cowboy swagger, step into **Kemo Sabe** (230 Bridge Street; 970-479-7474; kemosabe.com), known for its handmade Lucchese cowboy boots.

3 *Colorado Cuisine* 7 p.m.

Eating in Vail is not cheap. But that doesn't stop foodies from packing into **Restaurant Kelly Liken** (12 Vail Road; 970-479-0175; kellyliken.com; $$$-$$$$) for innovative regional fare. Menu items have included a rich elk carpaccio with mustard aioli, roast Colorado rack of lamb with mushroom bread pudding, and locally farmed bass with candied kumquats.

4 *Night Crawl* 9 p.m.

The party starts early in Vail—après-ski cocktails are at 4 p.m., which may explain why the town seems to shut down after dinner. A rollicking exception is the **Red Lion** (304 Bridge Street; 970-476-7676; theredlion.com), a dive bar packed with high-top tables. The entertainment tradition here includes performances by a guitarist and co-owner, Phil Long, that have included Bob Dylan covers, corny jokes, and Elton John sing-a-longs. If you're still wired, walk down the street to the candlelit **Samana Lounge** (228 Bridge Street; 970-476-3433; samanalounge.com), where 20-something snowboarders and South American lift operators pulse to the grooves of visiting D.J.'s.

SATURDAY

5 *Healthy Starter* 7:30 a.m.

Skiing at Vail takes lots of calories, so don't skip breakfast. For a civilized start, make your way to

Terra Bistro (352 East Meadow Drive; 970-476-6836; vailmountainlodge.com; $$), a sophisticated loft-style restaurant in the Vail Mountain Spa and Lodge that serves a delightful organic breakfast. Try the seven-grain hot cereal or cage-free scrambled eggs with potatoes and greens. If your objective is to get an early start, don't sit by the windows, where the snowy street scene induces lingering over cups of locally roasted coffee.

6 *Pick a Bowl* 8:30 a.m.

Skiing Vail's legendary back bowls requires a game plan, not only because of the travel time, which can run upwards of 30 minutes without traffic, but to avoid the morning crush. Aim to catch one of the first lifts to get atop the mountain ridge before everyone else. Expert skiers can claim first tracks on the extreme terrain at Sun Down Bowl, one of several south-facing slopes that make up the so-called backside of **Vail Mountain**. Try its aptly named neighbor Sun Up Bowl for the softest snow this time of day. Though most of the backside bowls are expert only, intermediate skiers are welcome at China Bowl, a gentler basin with wide-open expanses and panoramic views. Staying ahead of the crowds, push on to Blue Sky Basin, one ridge to the south. Hit the effervescent Champagne Glade before everybody else does.

7 *Unbuckle and Refuel* Noon

Relive your morning conquests at **Two Elk Restaurant** (970-754-4560; $$), Vail's flagship restaurant atop China Bowl. During lunch, skiers from the mountain's front and back sides meet here to unbuckle their boots and loosen their belts. Although the restaurant has 1,200 seats — all bordered by

ABOVE The lobby at the Arrabelle at Vail Square, a hotel in Lionshead, one of three base villages.

RIGHT Skating at Vail Square in Lionshead, on the rink near the Centre V restaurant.

massive timber-framed windows that overlook the Colorado Rockies — plan on getting there before 12:15 p.m. (alternatively, after 1:30 p.m.), or you'll be left standing. Service may be cafeteria style, but the fare is upscale. Dishes one chilly afternoon included chicken posole soup, buffalo chili, and portobello mushroom sandwiches.

8 *Long-Distance Cruising* 1:30 p.m.

Continue conquering the mountain in contrarian fashion, and skiing where the masses aren't. Now that the back bowls are brimming, point your skis toward Vail's front side, carved with many stamina-testing runs. By midafternoon, hit the four-mile-long Riva Ridge cruiser, the resort's longest trail.

9 *Muscle Relaxer* 4:30 p.m.

As the sun begins to dip and your muscles begin to tire, make your way to the Lionshead, one of Vail's three base villages, and check into the **RockResorts Spa** at the Arrabelle at Vail Square (675 Lionshead Place; 970-754-7754; arrabelle.rockresorts.com). You'll find separate men's and women's lounges, each with a steam room, a sauna, and a whirlpool. Treatments are mountain-themed: massages with pine-infused oils, body wraps incorporating wildflower essences. Therapists will even treat seriously sore muscles with an ice pack filled with mountain snow.

10 *High and Low* 7:30 p.m.

Still aching for more pampering? Stick around the Arrabelle for dinner at **Centre V** (970-754-7700;

$$$), a white-tablecloth restaurant that resembles a cozy Lyonnaise brasserie, with vaulted ceilings and a zinc bar. Indulge in French classics like steak frites and duck confit. Reservations recommended. But if you're hankering for more action—and to see Vail's scragglier, less effete side—drive eight miles to the **Minturn Saloon** (146 North Main Street; 970-827-5954; minturnsaloon.com; $$). This knotty-pine and antler-adorned place serves Tex-Mex dishes like chicken burritos as well as hunters' favorites like grilled quail.

SUNDAY

11 *A Walk in the Woods* 9:30 a.m.

In a ski town that lives and breathes sports, Olympic-caliber athletes are the real celebrities. So if you're planning to go snowshoeing, there's no better guide than Ellen Miller, the first North American woman to reach the summit of Mount Everest from both the north and south sides. Miller teaches a 90-minute Mountain Divas class at the **Vail Athletic Club** (352 East Meadow Drive; 970-476-7960; vailmountainlodge.com), which takes a crunchy cult of triathletes and trail racers on a valley trek through towering aspen forests, past trout-filled streams, and under snowy pine boughs. Unlike skiing, snowshoeing requires no special skills. Beginners, finally, are welcome.

ABOVE Belt buckles at Axel's, one of many shops in Vail that can supply the ingredients for an upscale cowboy look. Other stores carry luxe furnishings for your chalet.

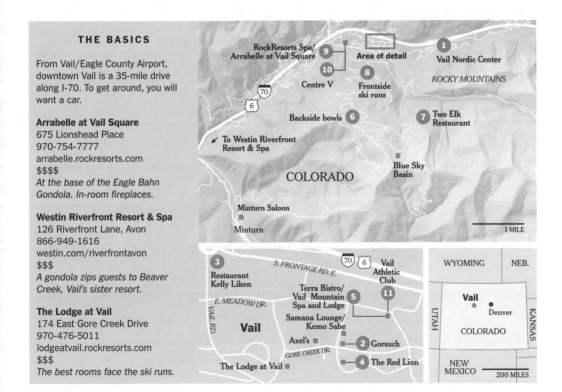

THE BASICS

From Vail/Eagle County Airport, downtown Vail is a 35-mile drive along I-70. To get around, you will want a car.

Arrabelle at Vail Square
675 Lionshead Place
970-754-7777
arrabelle.rockresorts.com
$$$$
At the base of the Eagle Bahn Gondola. In-room fireplaces.

Westin Riverfront Resort & Spa
126 Riverfront Lane, Avon
866-949-1616
westin.com/riverfrontavon
$$$
A gondola zips guests to Beaver Creek, Vail's sister resort.

The Lodge at Vail
174 East Gore Creek Drive
970-476-5011
lodgeatvail.rockresorts.com
$$$
The best rooms face the ski runs.

Aspen

At times Aspen, Colorado, verges on parody. Scoring reservations at the restaurant du jour requires the will of a tenacious personal assistant. Lines waiting to hand over black American Express cards for $1,000 Moncler jackets rival the ones for the Silver Queen gondola. Yet behind the mirrored aviator sunglasses is a culture devoted to the mountain's transcendent beauty and perpetual sporting life: skiing, boarding, hiking, snowshoeing, fly-fishing. Aspen is an international playground that remains a small town, one where it doesn't matter how much money you have, it matters how you handle a bump run.
— BY MARY BILLARD

FRIDAY

1 *Après Someone Else's Skiing* 5 p.m.

With alpenglow illuminating the Wheeler Opera House (1889) and the Elks Building dome (1891), saunter through this 19th-century Victorian mining town while enjoying the crisp mountain air and window shopping at stores like Fendi (fur flip-flops?). Though you didn't earn it, join the après ski action at the **39 Degrees Lounge** in the **Sky Hotel** (709 East Durant Avenue; 970-925-6760; theskyhotel.com), where a young, windburned crowd gathers by a crackling fire in wool hats to watch Teton Gravity

OPPOSITE Working the moguls at Aspen Highlands, with the Maroon Bells peaks in the background.

BELOW Cloud Nine Bistro, a good spot for lunch, is 100 yards below the Cloud Nine chair.

Research movies on flat-screen TVs. The footage of death-defying flips is a perfect way to get revved up. So are the drinks, including the Ménage à Trois, a mixologist's triumph combining vodka, double shots of espresso, and coffee beans.

2 *Chill over Chili* 7:30 p.m.

In the Roaring Fork Valley, billionaires aspire to be locals. Trade the *Us Weekly* setting for a more traditional down-home scene: the red-and-white-checked tablecloth décor at **Little Annie's Eating House** (517 East Hyman Avenue; 970-925-1098; littleannies.com; $$), an Aspen mainstay since 1972. Thick homemade soups, juicy burgers, and hearty chili are on the menu, as well as fresh trout. Everything goes with Fat Tire or Sunshine beer.

3 *Fresh Musical Tracks* 10 p.m.

Aspen offers a wide variety of night life in a few tightly packed streets, from South American frat-boy types playing pool at **Eric's Bar** (315 East Hyman Avenue; 970-920-1488; ericsbaraspen.com), to the fun-fur-wearing Euros at the members-only Caribou Club (caribouclub.com). But for live music go to the **Belly Up Aspen** (450 South Galena Street; 970-544-9800; bellyupaspen.com), formerly the Double Diamond. Ben Harper, the Flaming Lips, Ice-T, Stone Temple Pilots, and Dwight Yoakam have all played this 450-seat club.

SATURDAY

4 *Sunblock, Advil, Small Talk* 8 a.m.

To forestall the slight headache that may come with the high altitude (or a hangover), make a pit stop at **Carl's Pharmacy** (306 East Main Street; 970-925-3273) for a dose of small-town friendliness. Stocked with everything from hand warmers to wine, and open from 9 a.m. to 9 p.m., it is a place to trade gossip and feel at home. Even the out-of-town customers are Mayberry polite. And if you're buying a knee brace or reading glasses, someone will commiserate.

5 *Think about Seizing the Day* 8:30 a.m.

As you wait for the sun to soften up the snow from the overnight freeze, fuel up at **Paradise**

Bakery (320 South Galena Street; 970-925-7585; paradisebakery.com). Fresh muffins and something delicious from the coffee family are ready to be enjoyed while you sit on one of the outside benches facing the mountain. Read *The Aspen Times* and *The Aspen Daily News*, whose slogan is "If you don't want it printed, don't let it happen." Far from being resort boosters, the newspapers report on community concerns like seasonal workers and affordable housing and always have letters to the editor complaining about nearly everything. A town of millionaires shows its hippie heritage by still raging against the machine.

6 *Follow the Sun* 10 a.m.

Start with the legendary Ajax. The east-facing black runs — Walsh's or Kristi or the section called the Dumps — are best in the morning sun. **Bonnie's** (970-544-6252; $-$$) above Lift 3 is a must for lunch. Avoid the crowds by going before noon or after 1:30, and grab a spot on the deck. The staff makes everything from scratch, including the pizza dough. Look for warming choices like chicken artichoke chili pesto pizza and white-bean chili. The strudel is made with apples from a Colorado orchard, and it's best with fresh schlag. While some prefer the reserved seating of the members-only Aspen Mountain Club, there are plenty of captains of industry, Hollywood players, and members of the House of Saud carrying cafeteria trays. After lunch, hit the west-facing Face of Bell when the afternoon sun lights up the bumps and trees.

7 *Après Schussing, Shopping* 4 p.m.

Aspen has been called, and sometimes not so lovingly, Rodeo Drive East. The one global fashion temple to check out is **Prada** (312 South Galena Street; 970-925-7001), not only for its sleek

clothes, but also for the shop's rustic-chic modern mountain design of luxurious woods and stone. People frequently ask the name of the architect (Roberto Baciocchi of Arezzo, Italy). Then head to **Performance Ski** (408 South Hunter Street; 970-925-8657), where the co-owner Lee Keating and the latest crop of snowboard dudes will give you honest answers on how those Prada pants actually fit. A very pleasant place to curl up in an old leather club chair is **Explore Booksellers and Bistro** (221 East Main Street; 970-925-5336; explorebooksellers.com), a warren of book-laden rooms, a vegetarian restaurant, and a coffeehouse. For housewares, head to **Amen Wardy Home** (520 East Durant Avenue; 970-920-7700; amenwardy.com). The merchandise is so unusual (whimsical house gifts to fur blankets for a few thousand dollars), that it's worth shipping home.

8 *Spa Decadence* 6 p.m.

To take care of those aching muscles, hobble over to the 15,000-square-foot **Remède Spa** at the **St. Regis Resort** (315 East Dean Street; 970-920-6783; remede.com). It's pricey, but worth it. All treatments end with something that sounds a little zany but is actually relaxing: a stop at a cozy parlor where white-robed spagoers lie on chaise longues and strap on air masks, inhaling oxygen infused with fresh fruit essences. Prosecco and chocolates are also provided.

RIGHT Jogging past a Lamborghini. Behind the glitz and glamour, Aspen hides a real town of full-time residents.

9 *Did You Reserve Last Month?* 8 p.m.

The ski trails are never that crowded, even during school holidays, but trying to get a table for six at a hot Aspen restaurant is brutal. Two newcomers worth speed-dialing are out-of-towners with Italian cuisine. New York's famed **Il Mulino** (501 East Dean Street; 970-205-1000; ilmulino.com/aspen; $$$-$$$$) has old-school Italian pastas, fresh fish, and flirtatious waiters. Miami export **Casa Tua** (403 South Galena Street; 970-920-7277; $$$-$$$$) goes for a feel of an Italian Alps chalet.

SUNDAY

10 *Morning Tuneup* 8 a.m.

Stretch your muscles with a pre-ski yoga or pilates class at **O2Aspen** (500 West Main Street; 970-925-4002; 02aspen.com), in a beautifully renovated Victorian house. Drop-in classes are about $20. A small

boutique has everything from cashmere sweaters in the $500 range to more moderately priced workout wear.

11 *Bragging Rights* 10 a.m.

The cool kids tackle the Highland Bowl. It is not served by any lifts, and it takes anywhere from 20 minutes to an hour to climb 750 feet to its 12,392-foot-high summit with a fearsome 45-degree pitch. The really cool kids do circuits of two or three laps. Slightly tamer is Deep Temerity, a 180-acre bowl that gives expert skiers an additional 1,000-foot drop. Lunch at the aptly named **Cloud Nine Alpine Bistro** (970-544-3063) 100 yards below the Cloud Nine chair, with an old ski-hut feel and views of the Maroon Bells.

OPPOSITE ABOVE Downtown Aspen at dusk.

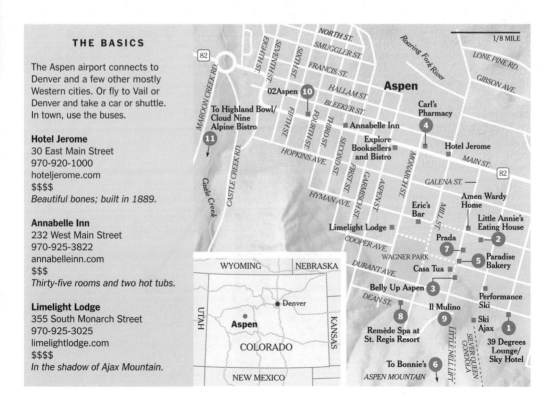

THE BASICS

The Aspen airport connects to Denver and a few other mostly Western cities. Or fly to Vail or Denver and take a car or shuttle. In town, use the buses.

Hotel Jerome
30 East Main Street
970-920-1000
hoteljerome.com
$$$$
Beautiful bones; built in 1889.

Annabelle Inn
232 West Main Street
970-925-3822
annabelleinn.com
$$$
Thirty-five rooms and two hot tubs.

Limelight Lodge
355 South Monarch Street
970-925-3025
limelightlodge.com
$$$$
In the shadow of Ajax Mountain.

Telluride

Telluride almost begs comparisons with Aspen. A Colorado mining town affixed to a world-class ski resort; rugged locals brushing elbows with the occasional celebrity; white-tablecloth restaurants serving up foie gras next to taco dives. "It's like Aspen was back in the '70s, but less pretentious," said Bo Bedford, a self-described Aspen refugee and a manager at the New Sheridan Hotel. "It hasn't gone Hollywood yet." There is, of course, a certain star-studded film festival. And Telluride does count Jerry Seinfeld and Tom Cruise among its regulars. Yet the town stays true to its hardscrabble roots. Dogs roam off-leash, folks rummage for freebies at a so-called Free Box, and residents zip up in flannel instead of fur coats. — BY LIONEL BEEHNER

FRIDAY

1 *Das Boot* 4 p.m.

Ski shops are often staffed by workers straight out of *Bill and Ted's Excellent Adventure*. Not **Boot Doctors** (650 Mountain Village Boulevard; 970-728-8954; bootdoctors.com), where Bob Gleason and his team of "surgeons" run a kind of operating room for your ill-fitting equipment. But don't expect a sterile ward — it looks more like a torture chamber, with pinchers and clawlike tools to stretch, squeeze, and custom-shape any size boots (prices range from about $20 for a boot stretch to $175 for a custom-molded sole).

2 *Broadway Meets Opry* 6 p.m.

Film and theater buffs will take comfort in Telluride's abundance of preserved art-house theaters. Take the intricately stenciled balcony and the maple floors of the **Sheridan Opera House** (110 North Oak Street; 970-728-6363; sheridanoperahouse.com), which dates from 1913. Part '30s vaudeville, part Grand Ole Opry, the stage has been graced with everything from Broadway musicals to bluegrass bands. It is also the hub of the Telluride Film Festival, which brings crowds to town each September.

3 *High Steaks* 8:30 p.m.

If the **New Sheridan** feels like the kind of joint with a secret poker game going on in a smoky backroom, well, that's because it is. (H. Norman Schwarzkopf

is said to be among the regulars.) But the real draw of this Victorian hotel is its newly refurbished **Chop House Restaurant** (233 West Colorado Avenue; 970-728-9100; newsheridan.com; $$$), which serves large platters of prime steaks. Like the hotel, which was reopened in 2008 after extensive renovations, the musty dining room has been spiffed up with plush booths and crystal chandeliers. After dinner, sneak away next door (there's a secret passage in the back) to the New Sheridan bar, which looks much as it did in 1895 — with its crackling fire and carved mahogany bar — but has added a billiard room in back and, yup, a poker table.

SATURDAY

4 *Biscuits and Gravy* 7:30 a.m.

With its red-checkered tablecloths and folksy service, **Maggie's Bakery** (300 West Colorado Avenue; 970-728-3334; $) holds its own against any ski-town greasy spoon. Start the day with a healthy-size biscuit and gravy.

5 *Gold Rush* 9 a.m.

Telluride feels as though it belongs in the Alps — with its 2,000-plus acres of backcountry-like terrain and above-the-tree-line chutes, European-style chalets, and snowy peaks framed by boxy

OPPOSITE Snow-carpeted trails roll past wide meadows and frozen waterfalls in the pocket of southwest Colorado around Telluride.

BELOW Alpino Vino has the feel of an Italian chalet.

canyons and craggy rock formations. Throw in thin crowds and short lift lines, and what's not to like? To warm up, take the Prospect Bowl Express over to Madison or Magnolia — gentle runs that weave through trees below the gaze of Bald Mountain. Or hop on the Gold Hill Express lift to find the mountain's newer expert terrain: Revelation Bowl. Hang a left off the top of the Revelation Lift to the Gold Hill Chutes (Nos. 2 to 5), said to be some of the steepest terrain in North America.

6 *Wine and Cheese* Noon

Telluride does not believe in summit cafeterias, at least not the traditional kind with long tables for diners and deep fryers in the kitchen. Its hilltop restaurants come the size of tree forts. Case in point is **Alpino Vino** (970-708-1120; $$), a spot just off the Gold Hill Express Lift that resembles a chalet airlifted from the Italian Alps. Diners in ski helmets huddle around cherry-wood tables and a roaring

ABOVE Downtown Telluride. Butch Cassidy robbed his first bank on Main Street in 1889.

OPPOSITE ABOVE The Gold Hill Chutes, some of the steepest terrain open to skiers in North America.

OPPOSITE BELOW A terrain park with an 18-foot-high half-pipe is illuminated by klieg lights.

fireplace, sipping Tuscan reds, while neatly groomed waiters bring plates of cured meats and fine cheeses. Arrive by noon, as this place fills up fast. For more casual grub, swing by **Giuseppe's** (970-728-7503; $) at the top of Lift 9, which stacks two shelves of Tabasco sauce and a refrigerator full of Fat Tire beer to go with home-style dishes like chicken and chorizo gumbo. After lunch, glide down See Forever, a long, winding trail that snakes all the way back to the village. Detour to Lift 9 if you want to burn off a few more calories.

7 *Full Pint or Halfpipe?* 5:30 p.m.

A free gondola links the historic town of Telluride with the faux-European base area known as Mountain Village. Just before sunset, hop off at the gondola's midstation, situated atop a ridge. For a civilized drink without cover bands, you'll find **Allred's** (970-728-7474; allredsrestaurant.com), a rustic-chic lodge with craft beers on tap. Grab a window seat for sunset views of the San Juan Mountains. Shaun White wannabes, however, will want to continue down to a new terrain park with an 18-foot-high halfpipe. Illuminated by klieg lights until 8 p.m., it is one of Colorado's few half-pipes where you can flip a McTwist under the stars.

8 *No Vegans* 8 p.m.

Carnivores should feel at home in Telluride. At some spots, steak knives look like machetes

and the beef is said to come from Ralph Lauren's nearby ranch. For tasty Colorado lamb chops, try the **Palmyra Restaurant** (136 Country Club Drive; 970-728-6800; thepeaksresort.com; $$$). Opened in 2009 at the Peaks Resort & Spa in Mountain Village, the glass-walled restaurant has dazzling fire features and romantic valley views. Or, for hearty grub you might find at a firehouse, head into town and loosen your belt at **Oak** (250 W. San Juan Avenue; 970-728-3985; $), a no-frills joint with old wooden tables and a counter where you can order Texas-style barbecued spareribs and breaded-to-order fried chicken.

9 *Getting High* 10 p.m.

If the high altitude and lack of oxygen leave you winded — and they probably will — pull up a bar stool at the **Bubble Lounge** (200 West Colorado Avenue; 970-728-9653; telluridebubblelounge.com), a grungy bar that serves craft beers, Champagne,

and, yes, oxygen. Choose from two dozen scents (cherry and lemon grass, among others) served in bubbling beakers that light up like DayGlo bulbs and look like something in a mad scientist's lab.

SUNDAY

10 *Stomping Grounds* 10 a.m.

The snow-carpeted trails that roll past wide meadows and frozen waterfalls in this pocket of southwest Colorado are ideal for snowshoeing. Stock up on snacks and water before riding to the top of Lift 10, where you'll find a warming teepee run by **Eco Adventures** (565 Mountain Village Boulevard; 970-728-7300). Eco offers guided snowshoe tours,

with ecological lessons thrown in, for under $50, including equipment.

11 *Outlaw Tour* 2 p.m.

Did you know that Butch Cassidy robbed his first bank on Main Street in 1889? Or that the town's red-light district once had 29 bordellos? These and other historical tidbits give Telluride an added sense of place that's missing from newer, corporate-run resorts. For an entertaining tour, contact **Ashley Boling** (970-728-6639; ashleyboling@gmail.com),

a D.J., actor, and self-appointed guide who offers 90-minute tours that are encyclopedic and long on stories ($20 a person; by reservation only). You may see him walking around town in his cowboy hat and red bandanna, guiding little knots of tourists and stopping every few minutes to say hello to friends — unless it's a powder day, in which case Telluride turns into a ghost town.

ABOVE The Bubble Lounge serves craft beers, organic wines, and oxygen. Telluride's altitude is 8,750 feet.

OPPOSITE Grab a window seat at Allred's for sunset views of the San Juan Mountains.

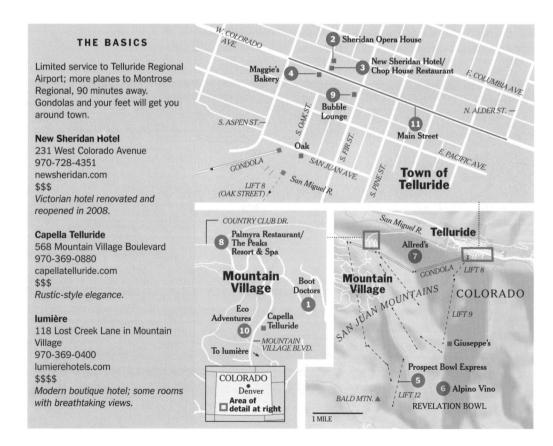

THE BASICS

Limited service to Telluride Regional Airport; more planes to Montrose Regional, 90 minutes away. Gondolas and your feet will get you around town.

New Sheridan Hotel
231 West Colorado Avenue
970-728-4351
newsheridan.com
$$$
Victorian hotel renovated and reopened in 2008.

Capella Telluride
568 Mountain Village Boulevard
970-369-0880
capellatelluride.com
$$$
Rustic-style elegance.

lumière
118 Lost Creek Lane in Mountain Village
970-369-0400
lumierehotels.com
$$$$
Modern boutique hotel; some rooms with breathtaking views.

W. COLORADO AVE.

2 Sheridan Opera House

Maggie's Bakery 4

3 New Sheridan Hotel/ Chop House Restaurant

E. COLUMBIA AVE.

S. ASPEN ST.

S. OAK ST.

9 Bubble Lounge

N. ALDER ST.

11 Main Street

Oak

S. FIR ST.

GONDOLA

SAN JUAN AVE.

San Miguel R.

S. PINE ST.

E. PACIFIC AVE.

Town of Telluride

LIFT 8 (OAK STREET)

COUNTRY CLUB DR.

8 Palmyra Restaurant/ The Peaks Resort & Spa

San Miguel R. **Telluride**

Allred's 7

Mountain Village

Boot Doctors

Mountain Village

1

Eco Adventures 10

Capella Telluride

GONDOLA LIFT 8

SAN JUAN MOUNTAINS

COLORADO

LIFT 9

Giuseppe's

— MOUNTAIN VILLAGE BLVD.

To lumière

Prospect Bowl Express

COLORADO
Denver
Area of detail at right

BALD MTN. ▲ LIFT 12

5

6 Alpino Vino

REVELATION BOWL

1 MILE

Santa Fe

The Plaza, the heart of old Santa Fe, New Mexico, hasn't changed much since the Spanish settled here 400 years ago, and it's possible to focus a trip entirely on the historic town center, where Native American handicrafts are for sale on every corner. But surrounding it is an increasingly cosmopolitan city. The rest of Santa Fe now offers groovy contemporary art spaces, hot Asian restaurants, and a park designed by a pair of trailblazing architects. Santa Fe is worth loving not just for what it was, but for what it is.
— BY FRED A. BERNSTEIN

apprenticed at the Eldorado Hotel and the Inn of the Anasazi — two local stalwarts — and made a brief appearance on *Iron Chef* before opening his own place, **Restaurant Martín** (526 Galisteo Street; 505-820-0919; restaurantmartinsantafe.com; $$), in 2009. The main draw is the food — dishes like ahi tuna tartare and duck breast with smoked bacon polenta and Marcona almonds offer hints of the Southwest, with a dash of global aspiration. But the homey décor makes you want to stick around even after finishing the bittersweet chocolate truffle cake.

FRIDAY

1 *Public Space* 5 p.m.

For a beautifully curated introduction to Santa Fe, visit the **New Mexico History Museum** (113 Lincoln Avenue; 505-476-5200; nmhistorymuseum.org), which opened in 2009 and includes a gripping display about Los Alamos, where the Manhattan Project was conducted in secret during World War II. A large courtyard with ancient walls and shady trees separates the museum from the Palace of the Governors (palaceofthegovernors.org), the Spanish seat of government in the early 1600s and now a small museum of Colonial and Native American history. The two-museum complex is free on Fridays from 5 to 8 p.m.

2 *White Walls and Wine* 7 p.m.

You'd have to be crazy to pay for a glass of white wine on Fridays. Canyon Road, which angles up from the center of town, has more than 100 galleries, and there are openings every Friday night. According to canyonroadarts.com, the largest category is contemporary representational (think brightly colored paintings of the desert). Check out **Eight Modern** (231 Delgado Street; 505-995-0231; eightmodern.net), where you'll find the geometric scrap-metal constructions of the Santa Fe artist Ted Larsen. The backyard sculpture garden is a great place to marvel at New Mexico's amazingly clear sky and savor its piñon-infused air before heading to dinner.

3 *Ahi Moment* 9 p.m.

Martín Rios is a hometown boy made good. Born in Mexico and raised in Santa Fe, he

SATURDAY

4 *Spice Market* 10 a.m.

The **Santa Fe Farmers' Market** (1607 Paseo de Peralta; 505-983-4098; santafefarmersmarket.com) dates back a half-century, but it stepped up a notch when it moved to a permanent building in 2008. Everything sold here, including dried chilies, yogurt, and grass-fed meats, is produced in northern New Mexico. The market is part of a bustling district that includes the new Railyard Park by the architect Frederic Schwartz and the landscape architect Ken Smith, both Manhattanites whose taste is anything but quaint. As you wander around, be on the lookout for the **Rail Runner** (nmrailrunner.com), a gleaming new passenger train scheduled to pull in from Albuquerque at 11:08 a.m.

OPPOSITE The Sangre de Cristo Mountains form a backdrop for residences designed by Ricardo Legorreta.

BELOW Don Gaspar Avenue in downtown Santa Fe.

5 *Sustainable Salads* Noon

Santa Fe residents care—as you learned roaming the Farmers' Market—where their food comes from. No wonder **Vinaigrette** (709 Don Cubero Alley; 505-820-9205; vinaigretteonline.com; $$) was an immediate hit when it opened in 2008. The brightly colored cafe has a menu based on organic greens grown in the nearby town of Nambé. Choose a base—Caesar, Cobb, and Greek are possibilities—then add diver scallops or hibiscus-cured duck confit. Add a glass of wine for a satisfying meal.

6 *Riding the Spur* 2 p.m.

Thanks to Santa Fe's sometimes depressing sprawl, it's getting harder and harder to find wide-open spaces. But drive (or bike) to the corner of

Galisteo Street and West Rodeo Road, where there's a small parking lot. Then begin pedaling due south, in the direction of Lamy (about 12 miles away). What starts as an asphalt path morphs into a dirt bike trail that swerves around a 19th-century rail spur. There are some pretty steep hills, but they're short, and the momentum from a downhill is usually enough to handle the next uphill. (If only life were like that!) The scenery is always gorgeous, especially in late afternoon, when the sun is low in the sky. **Mellow Velo** (621 Old Santa Fe Trail; 505-995-8356; mellowvelo.com) rents mountain bikes.

7 *Tapas With Strangers* 7 p.m.

La Boca (72 West Marcy Street; 505-982-3433; labocasf.com; $$) is one of downtown Santa Fe's most popular new restaurants—thanks to its contemporary tapas, plus larger dishes like cannelloni filled with crab, scallop, and Manchego. You'll find yourself sharing tips on what to order—and even forkfuls of delicious eats—with strangers.

8 *Reggae for All Ages* 10 p.m.

Santa Fe isn't a night-life town, but **Milagro 139** (139 West San Francisco Street; 505-995-0139; milagro139.com) is helping to change that. A building that had housed a coffee shop was recently converted to a restaurant that becomes a club on Friday and Saturday nights. There's no cover, and the drinks,

including a house margarita called Beginner's Luck, are delicious. A visit one summer evening coincided with performances by Rubixzu, a local band that performed a blend of reggae and Latin hip-hop to a diverse crowd, aged 9 to 90. For a trendier vibe, head to **Meow Wolf** (1800 Second Street; 505-204-4651; meowwolf.com), an alternative art space that is often open late during special exhibitions, or check its Web site for other parties hosted by Meow Wolf artists.

SUNDAY

9 *Free-Range Peacocks* 10 a.m.

For a big breakfast and an early start, drive south on Cerrillos Road about 10 miles past the Interstate, until you see a handwritten cardboard sign that reads, "Pine wood stove pellets sold here." You have arrived at the **San Marcos Café** (3877 State Road 14; 505-471-9298; $$). Dozens of peacocks, turkeys, and hens roam the property (which also houses a feed store), providing an Old MacDonald-like backdrop

for crowd-pleasers like eggs San Marcos, a cheese omelet in a bath of guacamole, beans, and salsa.

10 *Kitsch to Contemporary* Noon

If you ever thought that item you found at a roadside stand was one of a kind, **Jackalope** (2820

OPPOSITE ABOVE The Rail Runner train connects Santa Fe to Albuquerque.

OPPOSITE BELOW Desert, mountains, and Santa Fe.

ABOVE A touch of night life at Milagro 139.

BELOW The Santa Fe Farmers' Market. Everything sold at its stalls, including dried chilies, yogurt, and grass-fed meat, is produced in northern New Mexico.

Cerrillos Road; 505-471-8539; jackalope.com), a sprawling indoor-outdoor flea market, will disabuse you of that notion. There are hundreds of everything —look for items like punched-copper switch plates and tote bags that depict Michelle Obama smiling

ABOVE Revel in kitsch at the Jackalope, a sprawling indoor-outdoor flea market.

OPPOSITE Outside the San Marcos Café.

on a swing. If you need to shake off the kitsch, head to **SITE Santa Fe** (1606 Paseo De Peralta; 505-989-1199; sitesantafe.org), a contemporary art space.

11 *Bring Your Own Adobe* 1 p.m.

It's difficult to spend time in Santa Fe without thinking about buying a home (or second home) here. So check out **Zocalo** (Avenida Rincon; 505-986-0667; zocalosantafe.com), a striking development by the Mexican architect Ricardo Legorreta. He is known for crisp geometry and super-bright colors—a welcome sight in this city of browns and terra cottas. You don't really have to be in the mood to buy. Consider this real estate voyeurism, combined with a crash course in contemporary architecture.

THE BASICS

Santa Fe has a tiny airport with limited service. Most visitors fly into Albuquerque and drive about an hour to Santa Fe.

Hotel St. Francis
210 Don Gaspar Avenue
505-983-5700
hotelstfrancis.com
$$
Billed as the oldest hotel in Santa Fe. Fully renovated in 2009.

The El Rey Inn
1862 Cerrillos Road
505-982-1931
elreyinnsantafe.com
$$
Retro-chic 1930s-style motel with nicely furnished rooms.

Hilton Santa Fe Golf Resort & Spa
20 Buffalo Thunder Trail
505-455-5555
buffalothunderresort.com
$$
Part of a new casino complex 15 minutes north of town.

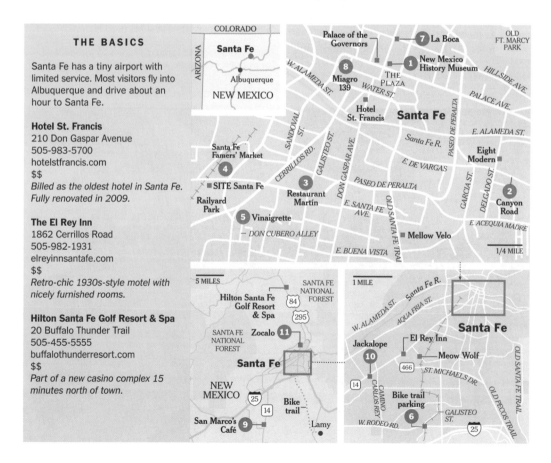

Albuquerque

New Mexico's biggest city has come back into its own. Thanks to tax breaks and great scenery, the TV and film industry is well established: scenes for Joss Whedon's mega-budget film The Avengers *were shot here, and TV watchers recognize Albuquerque as the backdrop for* Breaking Bad. *For visitors, the sprawl can seem daunting, but it is tempered by new bike paths. On the main drag, Central Avenue, neon signs from Route 66's heyday glow over revitalized, pedestrian-friendly neighborhoods. And along the banks of the Rio Grande, farmland provides a quiet oasis, not to mention heirloom beans, corn, and more to feed the city's vibrant organic movement.*
— BY ZORA O'NEILL

FRIDAY

1 *Mother Road* 3 p.m.

At night, Albuquerque's revived downtown can be a bleary seven-block bar crawl. By day, though, you can appreciate the ornate buildings financed by the railroad boom, like the exuberant Pueblo Deco-style **KiMo Theater** (423 Central Avenue Northwest; 505-768-3522; cabq.gov/kimo), which opened as a movie palace in 1927 and is now the city's public arts center. Enter through the business office to admire cow skull wall sconces and pueblo drum chandeliers. Nearby, drop in at classic shops like **Maisel's** (510 Central Avenue Southwest; 505-242-6526; skip-maisels.com), an emporium of American Indian crafts that's just the place to pick up a turquoise-and-silver bolo tie. Look for the '30s murals above the display windows, by artists from surrounding pueblos. **The Man's Hat Shop** (511 Central Avenue Northwest; 505-247-9605; manshatshop.com) is stacked to the ceiling with ten-gallons, fedoras, and more. A short drive south, stop off to see what's showing at the **National Hispanic Cultural Center** (1701 Fourth Street Southwest; 505-246-2261; nhccnm.org).

2 *Healing Potions* 6 p.m.

Go early to get a seat along the edge of the roof deck at the **Parq Central** hotel, a renovated 1926 hospital for railroad employees, tuberculosis patients, and the mentally ill. The menu at its **Apothecary Lounge** (806 Central Avenue Southeast; 505-242-0040; hotelparqcentral.com) notes the place is "not a

licensed pharmacy." Instead, it prescribes potions like a dreamy margarita made with prickly-pear juice and elderflower liqueur. As the sun sets, watch the east-side Sandia ("Watermelon") Mountains turn a luscious shade of pink.

3 *Home Grown* 8 p.m.

For a taste of old-school Albuquerque, head to **Golden Crown Panaderia** (1103 Mountain Road Northwest; 505-243-2424; goldencrown.biz; $), for empanadas, Mexican-style bolillos, and pizza with a crust of blue corn or green chili (or chile, as it's usually spelled in New Mexico). Salads are tossed with greens snipped from a tangled indoor garden. For dessert, get a classic anise-laced biscochito cookie and a double-shot espresso milkshake.

4 *Beer and Atmosphere* 10 p.m.

The drinking wing of **Marble Brewery** is called Marble Pub (111 Marble Street Northwest; 505-243-2739; marblebrewery.com), and it is a consummate New Mexican bar: benches, banjo players or salsa drummers, and lots of dogs. Rehydrate, after dancing, with a goblet of barrel-aged ale. Over in the Nob Hill district, east of the University of New Mexico, the longer-established brewpub **Kellys** (3222 Central Avenue Southeast; 505-262-2739; kellysbrewpub.com) is set in a 1939 Ford service station. Find a seat outside, weather permitting, by the vintage gas pumps and watch the fashion parade: flip-flops, graying ponytails, lavish tattoos.

SATURDAY

5 *Lucky Strike* 9 a.m.

In many cities, a bowling alley location, farm-to-table produce, and a chef-owner with Chez Panisse credentials would add up to hipster overload. But in Albuquerque, **Ezra's Place** (6132 Fourth Street Northwest; 505-344-1917; $$) is just another family restaurant, one of two run by Dennis Apodaca and his clan. A fluorescent-lighted room overlooking Lucky

OPPOSITE Hot-air balloon traffic is heaviest during the annual Albuquerque International Balloon Fiesta, but ballooning is popular all year round.

66 Lanes, Ezra's offers breakfasts like lacy blueberry pancakes with pine-nut butter and eclectic Mexican dishes like duck enchiladas with tomatillo-serrano salsa. **Sophia's Place** (6313 Fourth Street Northwest; 505-345-3935) has a similar menu, similar prices, and better lighting.

6 *Rolling on the River* 10:30 a.m.

Sixteen paved miles of biking bliss, the Paseo del Bosque trail in the city's lowlands hugs the Rio Grande. Pick up your wheels at **Stevie's Happy Bikes** (4583 Corrales Road; 505-897-7900; corralesbikeshop.com). Perhaps a retro three-speed tandem? Stevie can suggest a route, zigzagging along the tree-lined irrigation channels of Corrales, a village within the city, to reach the trail. One destination is **Los Poblanos Farm Shop** (4803 Rio Grande Boulevard Northwest;505-938-2192; lospoblanos.com), which stocks lavender soaps and salves.

7 *Clang, Clang, Clang* 3 p.m.

Even if a faux-trolley tour bus doesn't normally appeal to you, hop aboard the adobe-look **ABQ Trolley** (303 Romero Street Northwest; 505-240-8000; abqtrolley.com). The two owner-operators (one talks and the other drives and rings the bell) return happy waves from locals and blast Chuck Berry as they cruise Route 66. The tour features locations for *Breaking Bad* and tales of a young Bill Gates, who co-founded Microsoft here with Paul Allen before he moved back to Seattle. Special outings share Albuquerque lore in the form of talks on public art, ghost stories around Halloween, and tours to see holiday luminarias, the paper-bag lanterns that cast a glow on winter nights.

8 *Red Meat* 6 p.m.

Carne adovada — pork stewed in earthy New Mexican red chili — is the lifeblood of **Mary & Tito's** (2711 Fourth Street Northwest; 505-344-6266; $). Its recipe hasn't changed in decades, nor has its décor — the combination won it a James Beard

America's Classic award. Try the carne adovada as a turnover, wrapped in flaky dough and fried.

SUNDAY

9 *Up in the Air* 5:45 a.m.

Since 1972, when the first Balloon Fiesta convened, Albuquerque has been hot-air balloon heaven, with friendly winds and ample sunshine. Take a dawn flight with **Rainbow Ryders** (505-823-1111; rainbowryders.com). The bird's-eye view takes in the Sandias and dormant volcanoes, but most remarkable is the sensation of drifting just a few feet above the muddy waters of the Rio Grande. Your ride includes snacks and Champagne — a ballooning tradition, thanks to the sport's French roots — but you'll want to fortify yourself afterward at the **Grove** (600 Central Avenue Southeast; 505-248-9800; thegrovecafemarket.com; $). Go for pancakes with raspberry jam from a local farm or a chocolate-date scone.

10 *Church Music* 10 a.m.

Free espresso fuels the congregation at **Sunday Chatter** (at the Kosmos, 1715 Fifth Street Northwest; 505-234-4611; chatterchamber.org), a Sunday-morning chamber music and poetry series. Founded in 2008 by the cellist Felix Wurman, just two years before

his death, it was originally called the Church of Beethoven. Wurman's vision of a weekly ritual without the strictures of religion has become one of the city's best-loved musical events. Arrive early to score the best seats, a row of thrift shop easy chairs on one wall of the warehouse turned art space.

11 *Sweet and Hot* 1 p.m.

The decades-old **Frontier Restaurant** (2400 Central Avenue Southeast; 505-266-0550; frontierrestaurant.com; $) occupies the better part of a city block. The Frontier's walls are adorned with portraits of John Wayne, and its booths are occupied by every social stratum of the city. Standard order at the counter: breakfast burrito with bacon, fresh-squeezed

orange juice, and a killer sweet roll dripping with molten cinnamon goo. You can even take a frozen pint of New Mexico green chili home on the plane.

OPPOSITE ABOVE Anyone can leave happily with a fedora or 10-gallon hat from the Man's Hat Shop.

OPPOSITE BELOW Fresh baked at Golden Crown Panaderia.

ABOVE KiMo theater, designed in Pueblo Deco style.

THE BASICS

The Albuquerque International Sunport is about a 10-minute drive from downtown.

Los Poblanos Inn
4803 Rio Grande Boulevard Northwest
505-344-9297
lospoblanos.com
$$
Agriturismo, New Mexican style, set on an organic farm. Rooms balance brick and adobe with Alexander Girard textiles.

Andaluz
125 Second Street Northwest
505-242-9090
hotelandaluz.com
$$
Built in 1939 by the New Mexico native Conrad Hilton and recently renovated. Rooms have faux-Moorish doorways and Frette linens.

Böttger Mansion of Old Town
110 San Felipe Northwest
505-243-3639
bottger.com
$$
Victorian inn with period decorations.

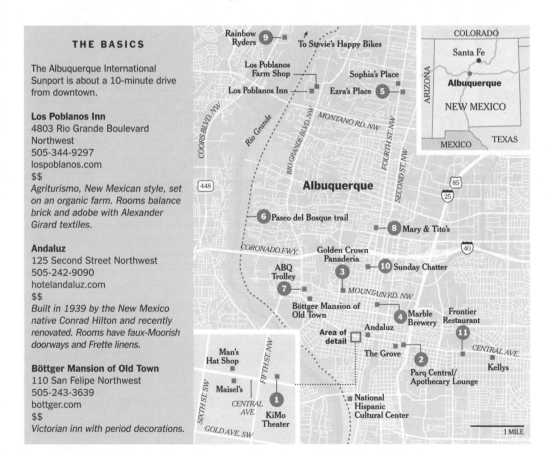

Dallas

Dallas may not be a world-class city, but it's pulling out all the stops to get there. Rich with oil money, it has pumped millions of dollars into civic projects, including the AT&T Performing Arts Center, a recent addition to the 68-acre Arts District. Meanwhile, glamorous subterranean bars and edgy Asian restaurants are giving the city a cosmopolitan aura. But when it comes to entertainment, its No. 1 attraction is still the Cowboys, now in their new, $1.2 billion football stadium featuring one of the largest retractable roofs and high-definition televisions in the world.
— BY LUISITA LOPEZ TORREGROSA

FRIDAY

1 *Architecture Park* 4 p.m.

See what Dallas is happily showing off these days. Go on a walking tour of the **Dallas Arts District** (artsdistrict.org), a 19-block area straddling downtown office skyscrapers and uptown luxury hotels. A prime attraction of the district is the **Performing Arts Center** (2403 Flora Street; 214-954-9925; dallasperformingarts.org), a four-venue complex for music, opera, theater, and dance in a parklike setting. A drum-shaped opera house was designed by Norman Foster and a cube-shaped theater is by Rem Koolhaas. To take it all in, find a bench at the **Nasher Sculpture Center** (2001 Flora Street; 214-242-5100; nashersculpturecenter.org), a museum designed by Renzo Piano with a lush garden that features works from a collection including Rodin, Henry Moore, and George Segal.

2 *Trend-Setter Cocktails* 7:30 p.m.

Size up the city's trend setters and assorted poseurs in their alligator boots and butter-soft tailored jackets at the **Rattlesnake Bar**, a plush lounge with mahogany-paneled walls and chocolate-brown leather sofas at the **Ritz-Carlton, Dallas** (2121 McKinney Avenue; 214-922-4848; ritzcarlton.com/dallas). Order the Dean's Margarita with organic

agave nectar, nibble on spring rolls with achiote pulled pork, and watch heads turn whenever a posse of lanky blondes in skinny jeans and designer heels sidles up to the bar.

3 *Southwest Supreme* 8 p.m.

Not so long ago, Dallas was a culinary wasteland, save for its famous barbecue. But in recent years, celebrity chefs like Nobu Matsuhisa, Tom Colicchio, and Charlie Palmer have planted their flags here, joining a fresh crop of hometown talent. At the top is **Fearing's** (2121 McKinney Avenue; 214-922-4848; fearingsrestaurant.com; $$$$), a casual but chic restaurant in the Ritz-Carlton that serves imaginative Southwest-rooted cuisine. Opened in 2007, Fearing's gained national acclaim at the time: Zagat named it No. 1 in domestic hotel dining, and Frank Bruni, the restaurant critic for *The New York Times*, called it one of the country's top 10 new restaurants outside of New York. Expect dishes like lobster coconut bisque and wood-grilled Australian lamb chops on pecorino polenta.

4 *Party High* 10:30 p.m.

There are still men's clubs, honky-tonks, and jukebox joints in Dallas, but the city's night life has gotten decidedly sleeker and flashier, with velvet-roped discos and bottle-service lounges. If you want a stellar view of the stars and the city's bright lights, go to

OPPOSITE Towers of downtown Dallas from the rooftop pool at the Joule hotel.

RIGHT Size up the city's trend setters and assorted poseurs in their alligator boots at the Rattlesnake Bar.

the rooftop bar of the **Joule** hotel (1530 Main Street; 214-748-1300; luxurycollection.com/joule). It features bedlike sofas and cocoonlike chairs arrayed along a slender, cantilevered swimming pool that juts out 10 stories above the sidewalk. Or, for an even better view, go to **FiveSixty**, Wolfgang Puck's Asian-style restaurant in the glowing ball atop the 560-feet-high **Reunion Tower** (300 Reunion Boulevard; 214-741-5560; wolfgangpuck.com). The rotating bar, which serves a dozen kinds of sake, offers magnificent views of a

ABOVE The Dallas Museum of Art, a city mainstay.

BELOW Forty Five Ten, the epitome of chic Dallas boutiques. The prices are shocking, but it's worth a visit.

skyline edged in colorful lights and the suburban sprawl beyond.

SATURDAY

5 *Morning Glory* 10 a.m.

Need a breath of fresh air after a late night out? Head to the **Katy Trail** (entrance at Knox Street at Abbott Avenue; 214-303-1180; katytraildallas.org), a 3.5-mile greenway that winds through the city's wooded parks and urban neighborhoods. Built along old railroad tracks, the trail is a favorite of young and old, bikers and runners, stroller-pushing parents and dog walkers.

6 *Slower Food* Noon

Chicken-fried everything may be a staple in Texas, but in Dallas organic salads and other light fare are just as popular. A trendy spot is **Rise No. 1** (5360 West Lovers Lane; 214-366-9900; risesouffle. com; $$), a charming bistro with a grass-green facade that serves up wonderful soufflés — a slow-paced antidote to Dallas's manic drive-and-shop lifestyle. Try the truffle-infused mushroom soufflé with a glass of dry white.

7 *Retail Overload* 2 p.m.

Shopping is a sport here, and there are more stores than just Neiman Marcus. For slow-paced window

shopping, stroll around **Inwood Village** (West Lovers Lane and Inwood Road; inwoodvillage.com), a landmark 1949 shopping center with an eclectic range of signature stores. Retail highlights include **Rich Hippie** (5350 West Lovers Lane, No. 127; 214-358-1968; richhippie.com) for retro and avant-garde clothing like a finely tooled pink leather jacket. Next door is **Haute Baby** (5350 West Lovers Lane, No. 128; 214-357-3068; hautebabydallas.com) for cute toddler wear. But perhaps the chicest boutique is **Forty Five Ten** (4510 McKinney Avenue; 214-559-4510; fortyfiveten.com). The prices are shocking but it's worth a visit. One shopper's finds included a vintage trolley case by Globe-Trotter and an iron vase by the Texan artist Jan Barboglio.

8 *Mex-Mex* 8:30 p.m.

One of the most popular Dallas spots for original Mexican fare is **La Duni Latin Cafe** (4620 McKinney Avenue; 214-520-7300; laduni.com; $$), which offers terrific dishes like tacos de picanha (beef loin strips on tortillas). For more inventive cuisine, try **Trece: Mexican Kitchen & Tequila Lounge** (4513 Travis Street; 214-780-1900; trecerestaurant.com; $$). The

formal dining room, dressed in cream, cacao, and sepia colors, invites celebration. Kick things off with a flavored caipirinha or a mojito before tucking into entrees like chipotle braised short ribs or vegetarian chile relleno.

9 *Cool Kids* 11:30 p.m.

Once a ramshackle district, the historic Cedar Springs neighborhood has a new energy, with gay-friendly discos, curio shops, burger bars, boutiques, and galleries. To mingle with the neighborhood's varied stripes, hit **J. R.'s Bar & Grill** (3923 Cedar Springs Road; 214-528-1004; partyattheblock.com), a cavernous club with brick walls, a tin ceiling, and a scuffed dance floor that draws gays, straights,

ABOVE Dallas Cowboys Stadium, the focus of most of the city's energy on home-game Sundays.

RIGHT Try authentic Mexican fare at La Duni Latin Cafe.

middle-aged couples, midnight cowboys, frat boys, and young ladies with thick makeup. Nothing gets going before midnight, when the pub crawlers and night lizards come out to play.

SUNDAY

10 *Sports Madness* 11:30 a.m.

If it's Sunday in Dallas, do as the locals do and hit a sports bar. There are dozens in town, if not

hundreds, but a favorite is the **McKinney Avenue Tavern** (2822 McKinney Avenue; 214-969-1984; mckinneyavenuetavern.com), affectionately nicknamed the Mat. There is a carved-wood bar with two dozen or so rickety tables fronting the 30-odd television screens that show nothing but sports, day and night. When the Cowboys play, the joint is bedlam. Rule No. 1: Go early, stay late.

ABOVE The Morton H. Meyerson Symphony Center in the 19-block Arts District.

OPPOSITE Fearing's, a chic, casual restaurant with imaginative Southwest-rooted cuisine. Celebrity chefs have planted their flags in Dallas, joining a fresh crop of hometown talent.

THE BASICS

Fly into busy Dallas-Fort Worth Regional Airport.

Rent a car for exploring.

Ritz-Carlton, Dallas
2121 McKinney Avenue
214-922-0200
ritzcarlton.com/dallas
$$$$
Reliable luxury, a fine restaurant, and a spa.

The Joule
1530 Main Street
214-748-1300
luxurycollection.com/joule
$$$$
Trendy spot with a jazzy basement nightclub, a Charlie Palmer restaurant, and a rooftop bar with a pool.

The Belmont
901 Fort Worth Avenue
866-870-8010
belmontdallas.com
$$
A moderate-priced alternative restored to bring back 1940s charm while providing modern amenities.

Katy Trail entrance at Knox St. **5**
To Rich Hippie/ Haute Baby
Trece: Mexican Kitchen & Tequila Lounge
8 La Duni Latin Cafe
Forty Five Ten
ABBOTT AVE.
KNOX ST.
PRESCOTT AVE.
WYCLIFF AVE.
DOUGLAS AVE.
AVONDALE AVE.
N. FITZHUGH AVE.
HENDERSON AVE.
CEDAR SPRINGS RD.
LEMMON AVE.
CEDAR SPRINGS
N
INWOOD RD.
6 Rise No. 1
LOVERS LN.
7 Inwood Village
J.R.'s Bar & Grill
BLACKBURN ST.
TRAVIS ST.
MCKINNEY AVE.
Dallas
DALLAS NORTH TOLLWAY
OAK LAWN AVE.
MAPLE AVE.
Dallas
KATY TRAIL
HALL ST.
75
Area of detail
10 McKinney Avenue Tavern
Rattlesnake Bar/ Ritz-Carlton, Dallas
MCKINNEY AVE.
2 Dallas Center for the Performing Arts
Five-Sixty/ Reunion Tower
The Belmont
2 MILES
DESIGN DISTRICT
N. HOUSTON ST.
Fearing's **3**
1
N. CENTRAL EXPWY.
35E
OLIVE ST.
FLORA ST.
ROSS AVE.
DALLAS ARTS DISTRICT
Nasher Sculpture Center
WOODALL RODGERS FWY.
The Joule **4**
MAIN ST.
COMMERCE ST.
1/2 MILE
OKLA.
N.M.
TEXAS **Dallas**
Austin • Houston
San Antonio
MEXICO
Gulf of Mexico

Fort Worth

How much art can you look at in one weekend? Of all American cities that might pose this dilemma, Fort Worth, Texas, traditionally a cow town overshadowed by neighboring Dallas, might be the least expected. But with oil-wealthy patrons eager to build its cultural endowment with sought-after artworks and interesting contemporary architecture to hold them, Fort Worth has become a place to go for art immersion. If you fear museum fatigue, take heart. The city's public art galleries don't overwhelm; they're on a uniformly intimate scale. And there's enough cowboy spirit left in town to give you a break from high culture whenever you want to take one. — BY RICHARD B. WOODWARD

FRIDAY

1 *Sundance* 5 p.m.

Fort Worth is dominated by a few families, none mightier than the billionaire Bass clan, famous for giving generously to George W. Bush's campaigns and for revitalizing the north end of the city. See some of their handiwork in **Sundance Square** (sundancesquare.com). Starting with two square blocks they bought in 1978, it has expanded to more than 35 square blocks dominated by a pair of Brutalist skyscrapers designed by Paul Rudolph in the '70s and now holding the headquarters of the Bass businesses. David Schwarz, the family's favorite architect, has contributed buildings in the Texas Deco style (blending Art Deco with state symbols like the star), including Bass Performance Hall, a home to opera, symphony, touring Broadway shows, and the quadrennial piano competition begun by and named after a local hero, Van Cliburn.

2 *Romance of the West* 6 p.m.

At the **Sid Richardson Museum** in the square (309 Main Street; 817-332-6554; sidrichardsonmuseum.org), take your time looking at the 38 oil paintings by Frederic Remington and Charles Russell. The museum displays only a tiny sample of the romantic taste of Sid Richardson, a millionaire oilman and Bass relative

OPPOSITE *High Desert Princess*, by Mehl Lawson, outside the National Cowgirl Museum and Hall of Fame.

RIGHT Breakfast at the Paris Coffee Shop.

who collected work on Indian and cowboy themes. If you'd like a different take on Western tradition, take a 10-minute drive to the **National Cowgirl Museum and Hall of Fame** (1720 Gendy Street; 817-336-4475; cowgirl.net), which celebrates Western women, from ranchers to celebrity pop stars.

3 *Saloon Chef* 7 p.m.

Chef Tim Love's **Lonesome Dove Western Bistro** (2406 North Main Street; 817-740-8810; lonesomedovebistro.com; $$$), near Fort Worth's traditional economic heart, the Stockyards, is a very modern pairing of *Iron Chef* cooking and cowboy chic. The decor is reminiscent of an Old West saloon, with a long bar and a tin ceiling, and the staff may be wearing cowboy hats. It's hard to say what the cattle drivers who used to come through Fort Worth would make of the cuisine, including dishes like a chili-rubbed pork chop with Yukon Gold-Swiss Chard Gratin and crispy onions, or beef tenderloin stuffed with garlic and accompanied by plaid hash and a Syrah demi-glace.

SATURDAY

4 *Breakfast for All* 9 a.m.

Don't be dismayed if there's a long line at the **Paris Coffee Shop** (704 West Magnolia Avenue; 817-335-2041; pariscoffeeshop.net; $). It seats more than 100, so tables turn over quickly. A Fort Worth institution since the Depression era, it seems to cater to everyone in town. Who could resist a place that offers green tea as well as cheese grits and has ads on the menu for everything from music lessons to bail bondsmen?

5 *Art of America* 10 a.m.

This is your day for serious art appreciation in the **Cultural District**, about five miles west of Sundance. Start at the **Amon Carter Museum of American Art** (3501 Camp Bowie Boulevard; 817-738-1933; cartermuseum.org). Carter, who made his fortune in newspapers and radio, was a Fort Worth booster who hated Dallas so much he reportedly carried his lunch when forced to visit, to keep from spending money there. His bequest financed what is now one of the leading collections of American art in the country, especially strong in Western paintings, 19th-century photographs, and Remington sculptures. The museum's original 1961 building by Philip Johnson was expanded in the late '90s.

6 *Art and Water* Noon

The **Modern Art Museum of Fort Worth** (3200 Darnell Street; 817-738-9215; the modern.org) has been an island of tranquility since it opened a new building in 2002. The architect, Tadao Ando, oriented the building around a shallow pool so that several of the wings extend outward and seem to float on the water. Have brunch at its **Café Modern** (817-840-2157; thecafemodern.com; $$), which attempts to serve dishes worthy of the setting—consider the Moroccan chicken salad or mushroom goat cheese crepes. Then explore the galleries, arrayed with a select group of postwar and contemporary works—usual suspects like Jackson Pollock and Dan Flavin, as well as rarities in American museums, like the German Minimalist sculptor Ulrich Rückriem. Whether in the sunlit bays beside the water, where you may find a lead floor piece by Carl Andre, or in a cul-de-sac where a wooden ladder-like sculpture by Martin Puryear reaches between floors, the building is still very much the star.

7 *Art and Light* 3 p.m.

The **Kimbell Art Museum** (3333 Camp Bowie Boulevard; 817-332-8451; kimbellart.org) provides an unrivaled museum experience combining first-rate architecture and first-rate art. From the street, the 1972 building, designed by Louis I. Kahn, offers a plain travertine exterior that will not prepare you for the

soaring harmonies inside. To step into the lobby is to enter a Romanesque church of a museum. Long slits and diffusing louvers in the barrel-vaulted ceiling allow the light to both cut spaces dramatically and softly spill over them. The collections, from all periods and places, are noteworthy for both aesthetic quality and historical depth. An 11th-century Cambodian statue of Siva is less a representative object than a stunningly beautiful one. European paintings — with masterpieces by Bellini, Mantegna, Caravaggio, Velázquez, de la Tour, Goya, Cézanne — are mostly presented without glass.

8 *Steak and Wine* 7 p.m.

You're not finished yet with cowboy-inspired cooking. **Reata** (310 Houston Street; 817-336-1009; reata.net; $$$) is Texas big, spread over several floors of an old building in the heart of Sundance Square. The fourth-floor bar has a panoramic skyline view. Reata's entrees run to steaks and chops, its wine list is extensive, and its desserts are tempting and calorie-laden.

9 *Hang with the Herd* 9 p.m.

Billy Bob's Texas (2520 Rodeo Plaza; 817-624-7117; billybobstexas.com), housed in a former cattle barn and touted as the world's largest honky-tonk, should be visited at least once, and perhaps only once. Walk around and select your entertainment option:

play pool or the 25-cent slot machines, watch live bull riding in a ring or sports on TV, eat barbecue or popcorn, shop for cowboy hats, try your luck at outmoded carnival games, drink at any of 32 bars, or dance and listen to country music on the two musical stages. A few hours at Billy Bob's may not measure up to an afternoon viewing Fort Worth's art collections. But as you merge with the herd (capacity is more

ABOVE AND OPPOSITE ABOVE The Modern Art Museum of Fort Worth, an island of tranquility that invites contemplation of both the architecture and the artworks.

BELOW AND OPPOSITE BELOW Pool playing and bull riding at Billy Bob's, an outsize honky-tonk in a former cattle barn. It can entertain 6,000 Texans at a time.

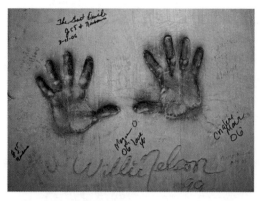

817-871-7686; fwbg.org), home to more than 2,500 species of native and exotic plants that flourish in its 23 specialty gardens. A favorite, the Japanese Garden, is a treat for the senses with koi-filled pools, stonework, and waterfalls. If it's springtime, expect flowering trees and migrating birds—perhaps, if you're lucky, a tree full of cedar waxwings on their way north.

than 6,000), sipping bourbon and watching the gliding two-steppers on the dance floor, it feels like a much more authentic and less imported experience —much more like Texas.

SUNDAY

10 *Texans Also Garden* 11 a.m.
Spend some peaceful hours at the **Fort Worth Botanic Garden** (3220 Botanic Garden Boulevard;

ABOVE Country musicians' handprints on the walls at Billy Bob's are Fort Worth's answer to movie stars' footprints in concrete in Hollywood. These were made by Willie Nelson.

OPPOSITE Texas exuberance on the dance floor.

THE BASICS

Fly into Dallas/Fort Worth International Airport.

Rent a car to get around.

Renaissance Worthington
200 Main Street
817-870-1000
marriott.com
$$$
In Sundance Square, with 474 rooms and 30 suites at a variety of prices.

The Ashton
610 Main Street
817-332-0100
theashtonhotel.com
$$
Attractive boutique hotel with 39 rooms.

Omni Fort Worth
1300 Houston Street
817-535-6664
omnihotels.com
$$$
Opened in 2009; skyline views and a rooftop garden.

Houston

A snarl of superhighways and skyscrapers, Houston is easily dismissed as a corporate campus — home to Fortune 500 giants like Halliburton and Waste Management and a company formerly known as Enron. Its generic towers sprawl to the horizon. The Johnson Space Center, where the world's eyes were fixed as NASA directed the moon landing from its control center, is 25 miles south of downtown. But this Texas megalopolis has been inching back to its urban core. Cool art galleries have sprung up in once blighted neighborhoods. Midcentury modern buildings have been saved and restored. And former factories have been turned into buzzing restaurants and bars.
— BY DENNY LEE

FRIDAY

1 *Park It Downtown* 5:30 p.m.

Houston may be a sea of office towers, but this subtropical city is also surprisingly green. Hundreds of parks carpet the city, and one of the newest, a 12-acre park called **Discovery Green** (discoverygreen.com), is quickly becoming the heart of the city's still sleepy downtown. Opened in 2008, the park serves as a true public space; elderly couples stroll around the artificial lake as toddlers roll down grassy knolls. For sunset cocktails, follow the area's young professionals to the **Grove** (1611 Lamar Street; 713-337-7321; thegrovehouston.com), a modern restaurant inside the park, which offers treehouse-like views of the skyline.

2 *Gulf of Tex-Mex* 8 p.m.

The city's young chefs are working overtime to step out of the shadow of Texas barbecue. Among the most feted these days is Bryan Caswell, the chef and owner of **Reef** (2600 Travis Street; 713-526-8282; reefhouston.com; $$), a seafood restaurant with a Southern twist. Housed in a former car dealership with soaring windows and ceilings, the restaurant creates a dramatic space for winning dishes like

OPPOSITE The Chapel of St. Basil, designed by Philip Johnson, is part of Houston's remarkable collection of midcentury modern architecture.

RIGHT A downtown view from the Grove restaurant.

roasted grouper with corn pudding and grilled peach. The dining room hums with an eclectic crowd — men in white suits eating ceviche, couples on dates, well-dressed families celebrating birthdays.

3 *Slice of Austin* 10 p.m.

Sports bars and mega-clubs fuel much of the city's night life, but a clutch of down-to-earth bars can be found along the tree-lined streets of Montrose. **Poison Girl** (1641 Westheimer Road; 713-527-9929) has pinball machines, a long shelf of whiskeys and a dirt-packed backyard jammed with 20-somethings in vintage Wranglers and Keds. Down the street is **Anvil Bar and Refuge** (1424 Westheimer Road; 713-523-1622; anvilhouston.com), which styles itself as a classic cocktail bar, though it can feel like a meat market on weekends. A handful of gay bars are also nearby, including the oldie but still rowdy **611 Hyde Park Pub** (611 Hyde Park Boulevard; 713-526-7070).

SATURDAY

4 *Drilling for Art* 11 a.m.

With all those petrodollars sloshing around, it's no surprise that contemporary art has an eager benefactor in Houston. The grande dame is still the **Menil Collection** (1515 Sul Ross Street; 713-525-9400; menil.org), opened in 1987 to house the

collection of Dominique de Menil, an heiress to an oil-equipment fortune. Blue-chip galleries include the **Devin Borden Hiram Butler Gallery** (4520 Blossom Street; 713-863-7097; dbhbg.com) and the **Sicardi Gallery** (2246 Richmond Avenue; 713-529-1313; sicardi.com). Scrappy artists, meanwhile, have carved out studios in downtown warehouses. Some of their work can be seen at the **Station Museum** (1502 Alabama Street; 713-529-6900; stationmuseum.com), which showcases emerging artists inside a big metal shed.

5 *Global Grills* 1:30 p.m.

While the city's sizable Vietnamese community is now scattered, traces of Little Saigon still remain in Midtown, a mixed-use neighborhood dotted with banh mi joints. A retro-favorite is **Cali Sandwich** (3030 Travis Street; 713-520-0710; $), a ho-hum cafeteria with 1970s-style vertical blinds and prices to match: the freshly made sandwiches include barbecue pork. If you're hankering for genuine Texas BBQ, drive north to **Pizzitola's Bar-B-Cue** (1703 Shepherd Drive;

713-227-2283; pizzitolas.com; $). It may not be as packed as Goode's barbecue empire, but Pizzitola's is the real deal, judging by the wood pits that have been charring ribs out back for 70-plus years.

6 *Pottery to Pinball* 3 p.m.

Malls rule in Houston—the biggest, the Galleria, offers 2.4 million square feet of brand names. Off-brand shopping requires a bit more driving. For one-of-a-kind home furnishings, head to **Found** (2422 Bartlett Street; No. 5; 713-522-9191; foundforthehome.com), which takes old industrial objects like hay feeders and turns them into architectural objets. **Sloan/Hall** (2620 Westheimer Road; 713-942-0202; sloanhall.com) carries an odd array of art books, bath products, and pottery—some by Texas artisans. **Peel** (4411 Montrose Boulevard, Suite 400; 713-520-8122; peelgallery.org) blurs the line between art gallery and jewelry boutique. And **Flashback Funtiques** (1627 Westheimer Road; 713-522-7900; flashbackfuntiques.net) is a trove of Lone Star Americana, like old pinball machines and gas pumps.

7 *Southwestern Redux* 7:30 p.m.

Robert Del Grande is considered culinary royalty here, credited with pioneering Southwestern cuisine in the 1980s. So when his restaurant of 29 years, Café Annie, closed in 2009, there was a collective grumble. The hunger was soon sated: he opened **RDG + Bar Annie** (1800 Post Oak Boulevard; 713-840-1111; rdgbarannie.com; $$-$$$), a multiplex of a restaurant with bars, lounges, and dining rooms that attracts a glamorous crowd that seems to favor short party dresses, shiny handbags, and aggressive amounts of gold. The menu is similarly bold and brash, with dishes like lobster meatballs with a rémoulade sauce and grilled rib-eye steak with a smoked Cheddar sauce.

ABOVE Brick-and-stone tradition at Rice University.

LEFT Sloan/Hall, a clever independent store on Westheimer Road.

8 *Two Dives* 10 p.m.

A party corridor has formed along Washington Avenue. A favorite among nearby bobos is **Max's Wine Dive** (4720 Washington Avenue; 713-880-8737; maxswinedive.com), with its long, inexpensive wine list. Seeking a different cast of characters? Night owls find the unmarked door that leads to **Marfreless** (2006 Peden Street; 713-528-0083; marfrelessbar.com), whose dark corners are popular with canoodling couples.

SUNDAY

9 *Bottomless Mimosas* 10 a.m.

A cafe tucked inside a nursery (it's called Thompson + Hanson) may sound precious, but so what? **Tiny Boxwood's** (3614 West Alabama Street; 713-622-4224; tinyboxwoods.com; $$) does a fantastic Sunday brunch. Situated close to the posh River Oaks neighborhood, the sun-washed dining room and vine-covered patio draw a handsome and self-assured crowd that mingles easily around a communal table. Chalkboard specials include leafy salads and a delicious breakfast pizza made with pancetta, goat cheese, and an egg, baked sunny side up in a wood oven. Pick up a cactus on the way out.

10 *Modernist Drive-By* Noon

Despite Houston's lack of zoning (or maybe because of it), the city has a remarkable collection of midcentury modern homes and office towers

ABOVE For one-of-a-kind home furnishings, head to Found, which turns old industrial objects into home décor items.

BELOW The Brochstein Pavilion at Rice University.

—some well maintained, others verging on collapse. Landmarks include the gridlike campus for the University of St. Thomas, designed by Philip Johnson. But many more are unknown, like the eerily abandoned **Central Square** building in downtown (2100 Travis Street) or the brawny **Willowick** tower, now condos, in River Oaks (2200 Willowick Road). Piece

ABOVE Cooling off at the Discovery Green park.

OPPOSITE Rice University balances its academic rigor with a richly decorated main campus.

together your own architectural tour with **Houston Mod** (houstonmod.org), a preservation group that maintains a resourceful Web site with Google maps and photos.

11 *Glass Houses* 2 p.m.

The skyline goes up, up, up every year. But notable architecture also takes place near the ground. The campus at **Rice University** — a neo-Byzantine maze of rose-hued brick and cloisters — got a new glass heart in 2008, when the **Brochstein Pavilion** (rice.edu/brochstein) opened near the central quad. A Kubrickesque box with floor-to-ceiling windows, it houses a cafe and media lounge, and has a fine-mesh trellis that extends like a mathematical plane in space. The structure is only one story, but it feels much taller —proof that not everything in Houston has to be big.

THE BASICS

Fly in and rent a car.

Hotel Zaza Houston
5701 Main Street
713-526-1991
hotelzazahouston.com
$$
Playful design and polished service in the lively Museum District.

Aloft Houston by the Galleria
5415 Westheimer Road
713-622-7010
alofthouston.com
$$
New with a pool and gym, in the Uptown district.

Hotel Icon
220 Main Street
713-224-4266
hotelicon.com
$$
A mix of boutique and classic hotel style.

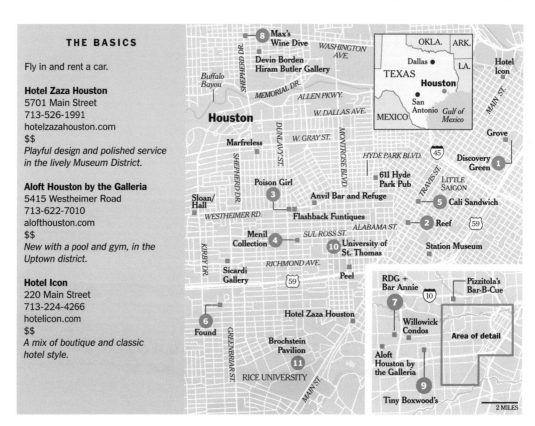

Austin

The unofficial motto of Austin, Texas, "Keep Austin Weird," blares from bumper stickers on BMWs and jalopies alike, on T-shirts worn by joggers along Lady Bird Lake, and in the windows of locally owned, chain-defying shops and restaurants. A college town known for its liberal leanings and rich music scene, Austin asserts its independent spirit in a largely conservative state. It clings to its tolerance of eccentricity in the face of rapid development including high-tech flagships and fleets of new high-rise condos downtown. And while its openhearted citizens, with their colorful bungalows and tattoos, continue to do their part, it has little to fear from encroachment of the staid and ordinary. As one local put it: "As long as Austinites keep decorating their bodies and cars, we're going to be fine." — BY JAIME GROSS

FRIDAY

1 *Dress the Part* 4 p.m.

If you forgot to pack your Western wear, make a beeline for **Heritage Boot** (1200 South Congress Avenue; 512-326-8577; heritageboot.com), where Jerome Ryan and his team of "boot elves" fashion fanciful boots out of exotic leathers like shark and caiman alligator, using vintage 1930s to '60s patterns. With colorful stitching, hand-tooling, and puffy inlays, they are instant collectors' items — priced from a few hundred dollars to around $2,000. For a less expensive route to the Texas look, stop by **Cream Vintage** (2532 Guadalupe Street; 512-474-8787; creamvintage.com) for vintage Western shirts and weathered concert tees, customized to your dimensions by an on-site tailor.

2 *Saucy Platters* 6:30 p.m.

Barbecue is a local sport, and there are a lot of competing choices. For a classic pit experience — meaning you can smell the smoke and sauce as soon as you pull into the state-fair-size parking lot — drive 25 miles southwest to the **Salt Lick** (18300 Farm to Market Road 1826, Driftwood; 512-858-4959; saltlickbbq.com; $$), settle in at a communal picnic table, and order the all-you-can-eat platter, piled high with brisket, ribs, and sausage. If you prefer to stay in downtown Austin, check out **Lambert's Downtown Barbecue** (401 West Second Street; 512-494-1500; lambertsaustin.com; $$). Carved out of a brick-walled

general store that dates from 1873, it is raising the bar (and provoking outrage among purists) with its newfangled "fancy barbecue" — think brown-sugar-and-coffee-rubbed brisket and maple-and-coriander-encrusted pork ribs.

3 *Fine Home for Fine Arts* 8 p.m.

Just off the south shore of Lady Bird Lake (named for Lady Bird Johnson, the former first lady) is the **Long Center for the Performing Arts** (701 West Riverside Drive; 512-457-5100; thelongcenter.org), opened in 2008 after an epic $80 million fund-raising effort. It has one of the largest, most acoustically perfect stages in Texas, home to the Austin Symphony, Austin Lyric Opera, and Ballet Austin. There's also a smaller black box theater spotlighting local musicians, improv troupes, and theater companies. Even if you don't attend a performance, it is worth stopping by for a glimpse of the glittering skyline views from the building's front terrace.

SATURDAY

4 *Start It Right with Tacos* 9 a.m.

Forget the oatmeal. In this town, morning means breakfast tacos, filled with scrambled eggs, potatoes, bacon, beans, and jalapenos in whichever combination you choose. Try them at **Tamale House** (5003 Airport Boulevard, also known as East 50th

OPPOSITE Cycling the Veloway in bluebonnet season.

BELOW Get your custom cowboy boots, crafted in traditional patterns, at Heritage Boot.

Street; 512-453-9842; $). It doesn't get more authentic, and it doesn't get more Austin.

5 *Bicycle Friendly* 10 a.m.

Explore the city at a leisurely pace by renting a bicycle from **Mellow Johnny's Bike Shop** (400 Nueces Street; 512-473-0222; mellowjohnnys.com), opened by Lance Armstrong, a native son, in 2008. In addition to selling and renting bikes, the shop stocks accessories like wicker baskets, messenger bags, and colorful racing jerseys. If you ask, staff members will chart an appealing route along Austin's 20 miles of urban hike-and-bike trails. A favorite is the **Veloway** (ci.austin.tx.us/parks/trails.htm), where cyclists roll past blooming bluebonnets in the spring.

6 *Munch and Browse* 2 p.m.

Some of Austin's best lunch food is dished out of Airstreams and food trucks by both amateur and professional chefs. You can look for a list on austinfoodcarts.com, or just be on the lookout as you explore South Congress, an appealing neighborhood for shopping or just window shopping. Find rare and collectible vinyl, from 99 cents to $1,000, at **Friends of Sound** (1704 South Congress Avenue; 512-447-1000; friendsofsound.com), down an alley off the main drag. Quirky souvenirs, like a duck decoy or beaver top hat, abound at **Uncommon Objects** (1512 South Congress Avenue; 512-442-4000; uncommonobjects.com), a sprawling emporium with a flea market aesthetic and a giant pink jackalope out front.

7 *Bats!* 7:30 p.m.

From early spring through late fall, the **Congress Avenue Bridge** hosts a Halloween-worthy spectacle: at dusk, more than a million Mexican free-tailed bats pour out from under the bridge and head east to scavenge for insects (austincityguide.com/content/congress-bridge-bats-austin.asp). The best spot for viewing the exodus is from the park at the southeastern end of the bridge, so you can see their flitting forms backlit by the glowing sky. To hear an estimate

of the bats' flight time on a particular evening, dial the bat hot line (512-416-5700, extension 3636), operated by *The Austin American-Statesman*.

8 *French Connection* 8:30 p.m.

There's something almost Felliniesque about driving down a dark road lined with industrial warehouses and stumbling onto **Justine's** (4710 East Fifth Street; 512-385-2900; justines1937.com; $$), a pitch-perfect French bistro. Outside, a family plays pétanque on the driveway; inside, groups of friends and couples sit on Thonet chairs at candlelit cast-iron-and-marble cafe tables as a turntable plays old jazz and reggae tunes. With atmosphere this good, the meal—Parisian comfort food, and delicious—is just a bonus.

9 *Performance Anxiety* 10 p.m.

The sheer quantity and variety of music in Austin on any given night can be daunting. Step One: consult Billsmap.com, which lists gigs everywhere in the city, highlights recommendations, and includes links to previous performances on YouTube. Two spots that reliably deliver a good time are the **Broken Spoke**, an old-time honky-tonk dance hall (3201 South Lamar Boulevard; 512-442-6189; brokenspokeaustintx.com), and the retro red-walled **Continental Club** (1315 South Congress Avenue; 512-441-2444; continentalclub.com), which dates from 1957 and has roots, blues, rockabilly, and country music.

SUNDAY

10 *Take a Dip* 10 a.m.

Wake up with a bracing swim in the natural, spring-fed **Barton Springs Pool** (2101 Barton Springs Road; 512-476-9044; ci.austin.tx.us/parks/bartonsprings.htm), a three-acre dammed pool that maintains a steady 68-degree temperature year-round. There's sunbathing (sometimes topless) on the grassy slopes, a springy diving board, and century-old pecan trees lining the banks. Afterward, park yourself out on the patio at **Perla's Seafood & Oyster Bar** (1400 South Congress Avenue; 512-291-7300; perlasaustin.com; $$) for a decadent lobster omelet and an oyster shooter spiked with rum and honeydew.

11 *Wildflower Country* 1 p.m.

Texas is proud of its masses of wildflowers, and you can find out why at the **Lady Bird Johnson Wildflower Preserve** (4801 La Crosse Avenue; 512-232-0100; wildflower.org), a University of Texas research center that is also a public botanical garden and spa. If you have more days to spend near Austin, or even if it has to wait until next time, follow the wildflower lovers southwest out of town into the beloved Hill Country. A region of rolling limestone hills, bloom-filled meadows, and dozens of wineries, it's the perfect next Texas stop, whether it's bluebonnet season or not.

OPPOSITE BELOW Saturday night at the Broken Spoke.

THE BASICS

Austin is served by major airlines and interstate highways. You will need a car or bicycle to explore the city.

Hotel Saint Cecilia
112 Academy Drive
512-852-2400
hotelsaintcecilia.com
$$$
Bungalows and five rooms in a Victorian house in South Congress. Amenities include a turntable in every room and vinyl records to play on them.

Hotel San José
1316 South Congress Avenue
512-852-2350
sanjosehotel.com
$$
Forty airy rooms simply adorned with Indian bedspreads and framed vintage concert posters.

Kimber Modern Hotel
110 The Circle
512-912-1046
kimbermodern.com
$$$
Six stylish rooms open to a patio shaded by a giant live oak.

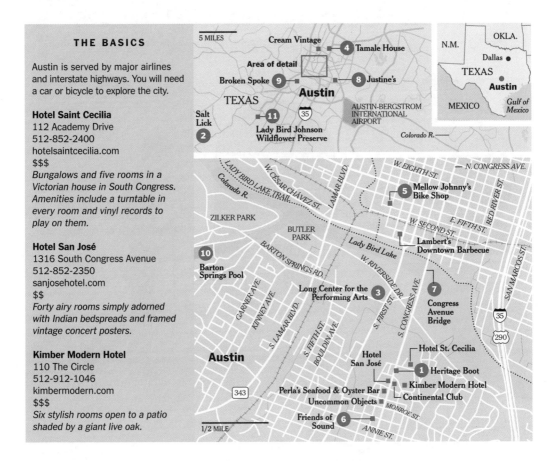

San Antonio

San Antonio, the United States' seventh-largest city, features a threesome of popular attractions: the River Walk (a meandering canal lined with restaurants and bars), Market Square (said to be the largest Mexican-style market outside of Mexico), and the Alamo (no explanation necessary). Beyond those obvious tourist stops, this old city also offers excellent Chicano art, 19th-century-style shopping, church music that goes way beyond hymns, and plenty of that famous Texas hospitality.

— BY DAN SALTZSTEIN

FRIDAY

1 *Shopping as It Was* 3 p.m.

La Villita historic district (South Alamo Street at East Nueva Street; lavillita.com), just off the River Walk, still feels like the little village it once was but is now crammed with artisanal shops, many of which are housed in lovely mid-19th-century buildings. The **Casa Clasal Copper Gallery** (Building No. 400; 210-271-3856; lavillita.com/copper) sells everything copper; a gorgeous set of hammered ewers started at about $40. **Alice Knight** (No. 1700; 210-930-5527; lavillita.com/aliceknight) sells Knight's playful and sometimes goofy paintings, as well as her delicate handmade-paper masks (from about $20). On one shopping day the artist's husband, Jack, was running the store. Is he an artist as well? "She lets me paint the edges," he said.

2 *Italy Comes to Texas* 5:30 p.m.

Five-thirty? What is this, the early-bird special? No, it's **Il Sogno Osteria** (Pearl Brewery Complex, 200 East Grayson Street; 210-212-4843; $$), and since it doesn't take reservations, the crowds line up early. The restaurant is Andrew Weissman's wildly successful Italian follow-up to his popular, now closed La Rêve. The industrial-chic space fills up with families and couples, some barside, gazing at the wood-burning oven in the open kitchen. Antipasti

included an addictive white bean purée, and the lasagna with wild mushrooms was a satisfying pasta option. The Nutella tart, a holdover from La Rêve, is achingly decadent.

3 *More Salsa* 9 p.m.

South Alamo Street, a short but colorful jumble of galleries, shops, and restaurants, is the main strip of the Southtown neighborhood, a diverse and welcoming pocket that's cherished by many locals. Let the beat and the warm bodies pull you into **Rosario's Café y Cantina** (910 South Alamo Street, 210-223-1806; rosariossa.com), a festive Mexican restaurant that pulsates with live salsa music and energetic dancing on Friday nights, especially on each month's First Friday, when the neighborhood sponsors a street fair of art and music. In a town famous for its margaritas, Rosario's are among the tastiest.

SATURDAY

4 *Brewery without Beer* 9:30 a.m.

Starting your Saturday at a brewery? Not to worry. Though it produced beer for over a century, **Pearl Brewery** (200 East Grayson Street; 210-212-7260; pearlbrewery.com) closed in 2001 and after an elaborate renovation reopened as a mixed-use complex. In addition to a few restaurants (Il Sogno included) and a branch of the Culinary Institute of America, there are a growing number of shops, including **Melissa Guerra** (210-293-3983; melissaguerra.com), a kitchenware store owned by the cookbook author, and the **Twig**

OPPOSITE Early morning at the Alamo, before the day's onslaught of eager tourist crowds.

RIGHT Museo Alameda, a Smithsonian affiliate, displays Latino and Chicano art.

Book Shop (210-826-6411; thetwig.booksense.com), an airy spot that offers a nice variety of best sellers and Texas-themed publications. There is also a Saturday-morning farmers' market (pearlfarmersmarket.com) with local vendors selling cheeses, salsa, herbs, nuts, baked goods, and all kinds of produce. Stroll and savor the aromas.

5 *Burgers with Conscience* Noon

Don't oversample at the market, because one of the more unusual dining places in town is a few minutes away in the Five Points neighborhood. **The Cove** (606 West Cypress Street; 210-227-2683; thecove.us; $) is a restaurant, car wash, coin laundry, and music spot. Its sloppy and satisfying Texas Burger (with refried beans, chips, grilled onion, avocado, and salsa) won mention in *Texas Monthly*. The Cove is also notable for its dedication to S.O.L. — sustainable, organic, local — ingredients, and it practices what it preaches with dishes like grilled tilapia tacos or a salad of roasted organic beets, goat cheese, and walnuts.

6 *Spirit of the Smithsonian* 2 p.m.

San Antonio has a broad visual art scene that ranges from contemporary to folk, with a special concentration on Latino work. There's a First Friday art walk (southtown.net); nonprofit centers like **Artpace** (artpace.org); and quality museums like the San Antonio Museum of Art and the Witte Museum. But it's **Museo Alameda** (101 South Santa Rosa Avenue; 210-299-4300; thealameda.org) that was chosen as the first official satellite of the Smithsonian. Alameda's hot-pink exterior belies the straightforward presentations of Latino and Chicano art inside.

ABOVE Creative decorating on the River Walk, the beloved pathway that snakes for four miles through downtown.

RIGHT The Cove, in the Five Points neighborhood, has an updated spin on familiar foods like hamburgers and tacos.

7 *Her Name Is Rio* 5 p.m.

After the Alamo, the most popular attraction in town is probably the **River Walk**, a four-mile stretch of paths that snakes through downtown along the canals (thesanantonioriverwalk.com). Sure, it's touristy, but if you avoid the often overpriced restaurants and bars that line it, a stroll can be lovely, particularly as the sun sets and hanging lights illuminate picturesque bridges.

8 *Eating Up North* 7 p.m.

To satisfy a Tex-Mex craving, head out of town to the Far North area, where you'll see the full extent of San Antonio's sprawl. Amid miles of highway loops, malls, and planned communities, find family-friendly **Aldaco's Stone Oak** (20079 Stone Oak Parkway; 210-494-0561; aldacos-stoneoak.com; $$), which serves up big portions in a large, noisy space. A patio looks toward Texas Hill Country. After your shrimp enchiladas, follow the green glow at Plaza Ciel, a nearby strip mall, to the **Green Lantern** (20626 Stone Oak Parkway; 210-497-3722), San Antonio's contribution to the speakeasy trend. There's no sign, but the low-lighted room and old-school drinks attract young professionals. Order something from the classics list, like a well-made Sazerac.

SUNDAY

9 *The Tourist's Mission* 10 a.m.

If you're a first-timer in San Antonio, or you just love the story of the Texans who fought to the death and want to hear it again, Sunday morning

RIGHT Mexican-American nostalgia in a Museo Alameda gift shop, inspired by a fondly remembered local botanica.

can be a good time to hit the **Alamo** (Alamo Plaza; thealamo.org). You won't lack for company — 2.5 million people a year visit this holiest of Texas civic shrines — and the parking may cost you. But the old walls are still there, and admission is free.

10 *Brisket Brunch* Noon

Texas' most beloved barbecue is served about an hour north in Hill Country, but the **Smokehouse** (3306 Roland Avenue; 210-333-9548; thesmokehousesa.com; $) represents San Antonio proudly. You'll smell the proof from the parking lot: this is the real deal. Friendly staff members work the 40-foot-long mesquite-wood pits. Order a sandwich or a platter by the pound, including the succulent, charred-on-the-outside brisket.

11 *For the Birds* 2 p.m.

Walk off those calories at **Brackenridge Park** (3910 North St. Mary's Street), a 340-plus-acre green space on the west side of town. The park's sunken Japanese Tea Garden offers a bit of serenity, while the bustling **San Antonio Zoo** (sazoo-aq.org) is particularly child-friendly, with a Lori Landing aviary where visitors can feed, and play with, brightly colored lorikeets. A different sort of Texas hospitality, but an entertaining one for sure.

THE BASICS

Major airlines serve San Antonio's busy airport. Rent a car at the airport.

Valencia Riverwalk
150 East Houston Street
866-842-0100
hotelvalencia-riverwalk.com
$$$
A friendly staff, comfortable beds, and valet parking offset the dark, moody décor.

Riverwalk Vista Bed & Breakfast
262 Losoya Street
210-223-3200
riverwalkvista.com
$$
Individually designed rooms in the historic Dullnig building.

JW Marriott San Antonio Hill Country Resort & Spa
23808 Resort Parkway
210-403-3434
jwsanantonio.com
$$$
Upscale accommodations.

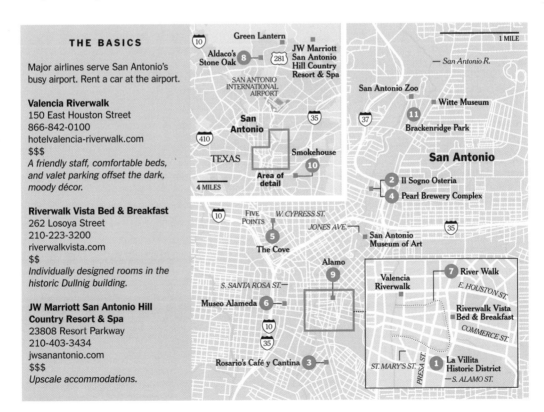

Indexes

Acknowledgments

We would like to thank everyone at *The New York Times* and at TASCHEN who contributed to the creation of this book.

For the book project itself, special recognition must go to Nina Wiener and Eric Schwartau at TASCHEN, the dedicated editor and assistant behind the scenes; to Natasha Perkel, the *Times* artist whose clear and elegantly crafted maps make the itineraries comprehensible; to Phyllis Collazo of the *Times* staff, whose photo editing gave the book its arresting images; and to Olimpia Zagnoli, whose illustrations and illustrated maps enliven every article and each regional introduction.

Guiding the deft and artful transformation of newspaper material to book form at TASCHEN were Marco Zivny, the book's designer; Josh Baker, the art director; and Jennifer Patrick, production manager. Also at TASCHEN, David Martinez, Jessica Sappenfeld, Anna-Tina Kessler, Kirstin Plate and Janet Kim provided production assistance, and at the *Times*, Heidi Giovine helped at critical moments. Craig B. Gaines copy-edited the manuscript.

But the indebtedness goes much further back. This book grew out of the work of all of the editors, writers, photographers, and *Times* staff people whose contributions and support for the weekly "36 Hours" column built a rich archive over many years.

For this legacy, credit must go first to Stuart Emmrich, who created the column in 2002 and then refined the concept and guided its development over eight years, first as the *Times* Escapes editor and then as Travel editor. Without his vision, there would be no "36 Hours."

Great thanks must go to all of the writers and photographers whose work appears in the book, both *Times* staffers and freelancers.

And a legion of *Times* editors behind the scenes made it all happen, and still do.

Danielle Mattoon, who took over as Travel editor in 2010, has brought her steady hand to "36 Hours," and found time to be supportive of this book as well.

Suzanne MacNeille, now the column's direct editor, and her predecessors Jeff Z. Klein and Denny Lee have all superbly filled the role of finding and working with writers, choosing and assigning destinations, and assuring that the weekly product would entertain and inform readers while upholding *Times* journalistic standards. The former Escapes editors Amy Virshup and Mervyn Rothstein saw the column through many of its early years, assuring its consistent quality.

The talented *Times* photo editors who have overseen images and directed the work of the column's photographers include Lonnie Schlein, Jessica DeWitt, Gina Privitere, Darcy Eveleigh, Laura O'Neill, Chris Jones, and the late John Forbes. The newspaper column's design is the work of the *Times* art director Rodrigo Honeywell.

Among the many editors on the *Times* Travel and Escapes copy desks who have kept "36 Hours" at its best over the years, three who stand out are Florence Stickney, Steve Bailey, and Carl Sommers. Editors of the column on the *New York Times* web site have been Alice Dubois, David Allan, Miki Meek, Allison Busacca, and Danielle Belopotosky. Much of the fact-checking, that most invaluable and unsung of skills, was in the hands of Rusha Haljuci, Nick Kaye, Anna Bahney, and George Gustines.

Finally, we must offer a special acknowledgment to Benedikt Taschen, whose longtime readership and interest in the "36 Hours" column led to the partnership of our two companies to produce this book.

— BARBARA IRELAND AND ALEX WARD

Copyright © 2013 *The New York Times*. All Rights Reserved.

Editor Barbara Ireland
Project management Alex Ward
Photo editor Phyllis Collazo
Maps Natasha Perkel
Spot illustrations and region maps Olimpia Zagnoli
Editorial coordination Nina Wiener and Eric Schwartau
Art direction Marco Zivny and Josh Baker
Layout and design Marco Zivny
Production Jennifer Patrick

To stay informed about upcoming TASCHEN titles, please request our magazine at www.taschen.com/magazine or write to TASCHEN, Hohenzollernring 53, D–50672 Cologne, Germany, contact@taschen.com. We will be happy to send you a free copy of our magazine which is filled with information about all of our books.

©2013 TASCHEN GmbH
Hohenzollernring 53, D–50672 Köln, www.taschen.com

ISBN 978-3-8365-4203-6 Printed in China

TRUST *THE NEW YORK TIMES* WITH YOUR NEXT 36 HOURS

"An elegant... planning tool and beautifully photographed coffee-table book."

—FORBES.COM, *NEW YORK*

USA & CANADA*
* also available for iPad and iPhone

EUROPE*

LATIN AMERICA & THE CARIBBEAN

ASIA & OCEANIA

USA & CANADA REGION BY REGION

NORTHEAST

SOUTHEAST

MIDWEST & GREAT LAKES

SOUTHWEST & ROCKY MOUNTAINS

WEST COAST